Colorado Coach Diary I

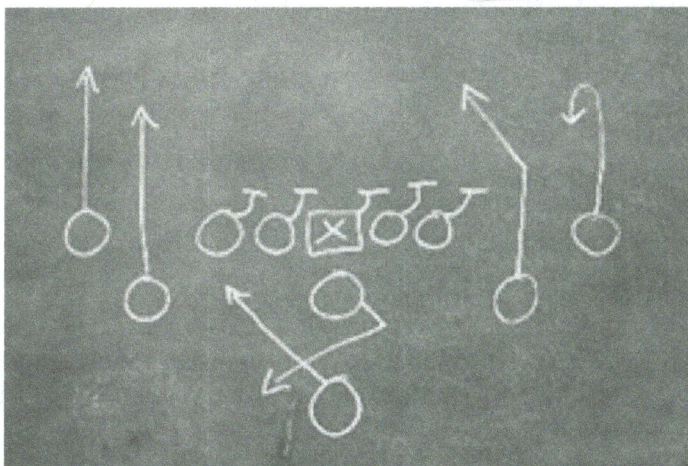

Colorado Coach Diary I
Author: chrmd
First printing
Printed in the United States of America
Copyright © 2025 chrmd
ISBN: 979-8-218-81894-4
Graphic Design: Stephanie Gamez
DoctorOfSports.com

Characters

A) Wilford Tremby: Highly successful high school coach in Chicago who moves to North Colorado Springs to coach a new school (Colorado Sports Academy High School). Now a young widower.

B) Janae Tremby: Deceased Wife from metastatic breast cancer who succumbs just prior to move.

C) Josh, Jake, Jaiden Tremby: (3 young Tremby boys)

D) Missy Bradford: Attractive Denver newspaper sports reporter

E) Dr. Alison Maples: Pediatrician girlfriend

F) Sherry and Herb Tompkins: Janae Tremby's parents living in Greenfield Village, Colorado

G) Smitty: Colorful sports loving nosy neighbor

H) Mandy Nelson: Attractive millennial Jewish debutante lady Coach Wilford Tremby meets at a "Coming Out" party in Greenfield Village, Colorado (home of Janae Tremby's parents)

Prologue

"Colorado Coach Diary I" is a podcast and book that offers an inside "real-life" look at the life of an excellent high school English, Literature, and Composition instructor and football coach. The Colorado Coach Diary I specifically shares a young football coach's insight about his personal and professional life. The podcast and diary book are hosted by a now – widowed highly successful football coach. Coach Wilford Tremby discusses balancing coaching duties with family obligations (3 young boys), game strategy preparation, and personal growth through new Colorado relationships and ongoing resolution of severe grief from his beautiful wife's untimely death.

Colorado Coach Diary I explores the challenges of coaching, personal anecdotes, and professional responsibilities - providing a relatable narrative for listeners interested in sports commentary and personal reflection. Poignant aspects of Colorado living, culture, and intriguing football coaching and teacher challenges await the reader. Sports fans will love the novel football plays and schemes introduced; while a widower's life and love story weaves through the diary days.

You can find "Colorado Coach Diary" on podcast platforms like Podcast Republic, Songkick, Spotify, Pod bean, and Apple Podcasts. The podcast is available for download, and listeners can also access episode descriptions and transcripts. The book is available on Amazon and other book outlets.

Day 1

I cannot believe we finally arrived in Colorado. This is the most difficult part of my life I will ever experience. Thankfully, my three boys Josh, Jake, and Jaiden are all doing well with the move from inner city Chicago. The neighbors in North Colorado Springs have helped immensely along with the school administrators and teachers. Josh just turned 5, Jake is 3 and Jaiden 1. Josh starts kindergarten tomorrow in District 38 at a Charter School – tough to enroll especially if you do not know the environment or have a family history. We are completely unknown with a relatively new house purchased from the bank under a foreclosure sale. Everything on the house was completed including landscaping. The owner had to bail due to illness. I offered to let him stay for a period; but he moved out of state into a relative's basement. Our kids already have friends within 24 hours and they are playing hide and seek with a large group of kids. Jaiden just began walking so he is not competitive – though he thinks he is a serious player. The weather is perfect and I can see Pikes Peak with a small amount of snow. Some of our belongings are yet to arrive; and we are sleeping on mattresses in the living room. The kids surround me and we have been sleeping on one mattress.

Josh asks when mommy is coming back. Jake says mom constantly; and Jaiden mutters mom also – like mummy. I frankly need a counselor for me to help with the kids and explain what has happened. We drove from Chicago; and the kids assumed mom was coming later despite me informing them otherwise. It is hard not to break out in flowing tears like Niagara Falls. I am trying to not talk on my iPhone to friends and family when the kids are around; but it is difficult. I am hearing constantly from administrators, coaches, parents, family, and the Colorado High School Athletic Association endlessly. There seem to be more school and athletic rules about everything in the day and age of political correctness, gender disorientation, participation trophy culture and grade inflation. The administrators, coaches, and parents have warned me already about pressure to allow bad-grade players to play, transgender kids wanting on the team, and potential drug issues in Colorado – like THC/fentanyl/methamphetamine. I do not expect my players to be angels; but, if they want to play, they will abide by the rules. This is a great opportunity and Colorado Sports Academy High School to have winning teams.

I have been assigned English class. My English classes will be strict and fundamental. I will begin with middle school basics and advance to college level English. All students will be required to know 100% of the material; and I expect all of them to master the real language from its primordial origins. I want learning to be fun and productive. Expectations will be for my classes to master all the material and advance onto college, military, or trade school. I have added phonics and cursive to the curriculum at my discretion. There will be days without computers and iPhone in my class. I informed the school, parents, and coaches regarding my strictness with coaching and English instruction. The transgender issue will be followed by CHSA rules which states that the school will determine the appropriate gender assignment for sports participation. I am not sweating this since I highly respect transgenders. If we have a transitioned biological

4

girl playing football, I will meet with the family, physician, and administrators individually to ensure we are on the same page regarding risks and other issues (like bathrooms). I will ensure safety and privacy for all students. I dealt with this issue in Chicago; and it was not a big deal.

My football practices at Colorado Sports Academy High School will be quite rugged. Two-a-days with one session film and bulletin board coaching fundamentals in street clothes will occur. Most of these athletes transferring into Colorado Sports Academy High School will be instructed that every position is competitive; and practice and play will determine the depth chart. The expectations for our new school (Colorado Sports Academy High School) are quite high. I have been interviewed when I walked onto our new property by The Denver Post, KOA radio, and even ESPN. Our school will play 5A in all sports due to our high enrollment (> 939 students). I like the competition along the front range; but expectedly we will be playing elite schools with a winning legacy and culture. Though I was successful in Chicago and had offers throughout the United States for taking a beleaguered inner City Chicago team to the state championship, I have an uphill fight in all the sports I will coach - including football, basketball, and golf. My salary has doubled; but my stress has quadrupled.

Janae, my wife, left our world early. We tried every imaginable treatment for her metastatic and painful breast cancer. Nothing worked and she just worsened clinically. The home hospice was very difficult on the kids because none of them understood the gravity of Mom's fatal illness. I needed to provide her morphine constantly to barely dull the pain. It required her to be asleep nearly 24/7. We discussed delaying the Colorado move for a year; but she insisted the job would not be open. Janae wanted to move back home to Colorado and have our kids experience skiing, hockey, and fly-fishing. We kept hoping she would improve and rid her body of this scourge. Despite the illness, Janae made me promise to take the job, move, and love our kids. It is difficult for myself to go on; but I am doing this out of total respect for my wife. Staying in Chicago I would have had day care, a nanny, a winning team, and plenty of perks. Finishing settling Janae's estate after the funeral and dealing with endless amounts of family affairs with small kids was difficult. Thankfully, it was during the summer and I had time to deal with Janae's death. Colorado is a new start; and I will move on per Janae's directive. I will survive. Janae made me promise to write a diary and publish it in her honor - perhaps do a podcast. I love English, cursive, and writing. I will "flatout" do it in her honor.

Day 2

I received a call from an assistant coach in Denver who removed himself from the Denver Cherry Preparatory High School coaching squad due to an incident with a girls track team. He is an excellent and renown coach in many high school sports. A female track star accused him of discrimination and playing favorites after she was removed from a relay team. The Cherry Preparatory School District met; and before the hearing was completed, the coach decided he would leave to find another opportunity. The school released him with a mutual release and severance with no further hearings or litigation planned. The gal on the track squad later admitted she lied and she was appropriately demoted due to slower track times and not discrimination. Her times in the 100 meters had fallen to 5th on the team. Thus, she was made a substitute and trained with the team daily. Previously, she had been the anchor of this state winning girls 4x100 relay team. Now I have got my first mess. I would like to hire this guy (Hal Stevens) to begin with football. I do not want distractions nor the media following our team and him around looking for creative journalism. I want our squad to be about winning football; not personal matters or enlightened gossip. Thus, I will discuss this with the school board and Superintendent. The school has provided myself free reign over the hiring and firing of coaches as I am also the athletic director. They have combined the positions for now to save on salaries and duplication. My 6-figure salary is enough for me to survive and maintain a family. I am wading water somewhat, nervous, and anxious about the future. I would have stayed in Chicago if Janae had not made me promise her to raise our kids in Colorado. I will make the best of the situation.

Janae's parents live in Greenwood Village – the upper crust area of Denver. Janae detested some of her family's wealth; but was close to her parents. I get along great with her parents (Sherry and Herb Tompkins). They were successful oil shale business partners and sold their company to a conglomerate for a wonderful parachute at the end of their career. They love sports and loved me because I was a coach. Janae and I met at a turn style in Soldier Field. She was an accountant for the Wrigley Family. Janae's perk was two free Bears tickets. She was running out of Soldier Field and her lengthy purse caught on the turn style. Janae fell to the ground in an awkward position. I thought she really hurt herself. Janae was more shocked than hurt. Her supposed boyfriend just stared and essentially did zero. I helped her to her feet and she smiled at me and frowned at the boyfriend. We talked for a minute as I picked up her coat, purse belongings and said good-bye.

I never thought anything about her until at the end of football practice two days later she revealed herself and asked if she could observe. After I recognized Janae, I informed her if she was not a spy from a neighboring competitor; it was okay to watch. Recording on her iPhone was not allowed. She wanted to thank me for picking her up at Soldier Field. I felt it was the right thing to do; and it was not that big of a deal. I asked her how she found me. Janae said I had a shirt on that read Manion Prep Coaching. Her office is not far from the practice field near downtown Chicago. She wanted to thank me by purchasing supper at a nearby café. I said this was satisfactory and would work. Unfortunately, I had an injured player that needed an orthopedist tonight. I was taking him to Cook County ER. She then asked if she could tag along; and I agreed. I met his parents there and it revealed an ankle fracture requiring a pin the following morning – season over for our starting tailback. The parents took him home and Janae and I late traveled to the hospital cafeteria for my "thank you" supper.

Janae basically dumped her boyfriend the day after the incident at Soldier Field. Janae and I never really dated and fell in love apparently at Soldier Field. We meshed with friends, coaches, families, and jobs. Janae always made football practices as our team won the most competitive class state high school football (5A). She had more fun spectating than I did coaching. She missed a monthly period, I proposed, and we were married 3 months after we met. I was extremely fortunate in finding such a great all-around spouse. Janae knew what she wanted. She strongly desired kids, Colorado, and me. I felt fortunate in having a beautiful blue-eyed Catholic blond chasing me. My family in Chicago loved Janae. Janae loved all my Tremby brothers, sisters, and parents. We all "got along" well and saw each other frequently. Janae loved that my family was middle class and lived-in inner-city Chicago. Underneath, my mother was worried about us leaving for Colorado and the 1000-mile separation. Mom loved the grandchildren and was a worthy frequent baby-sitter. Dad also helped a ton. Now, I am on my own living in Colorado and living out Janae's dream.

My in-laws, Sherry, and Herb Tompkins, have been down to see the grandkids some; and it has gone reasonably well. Sherry (Mom-in-law) has already intimated that she has completed scouting and background checks on available "suitable" women in her area. I am under-reacting to all this surrounding fluffiness. I am not even close to another relationship, want to concentrate on coaching and the kids, and barely have enough time to get my work as AD completed (hiring a girl's JV volleyball coach in the morning if all goes well). I am trying to be nice; and will fend off Janae's mom from diverting my focus on coaching. I could lose all 12 games this year and be media, parent, and player blasted…potentially removed. This school is an experiment for the Colorado Springs area to attract great student athletes and compete against Denver superiority on the athletic and academic fields. Sunday afternoons I will be diagramming plays instead of sitting in a girlfriend's living room in Greenwood Village with everyone staring and evaluating me. I am a guy and a coach…now a parent. I can figure life out without intrusions; and I do not need another distraction in my life. Perhaps in a few months, I can date, but, assuredly, not now. The phone is ringing with the district superintendent on the phone about hiring Coach Stevens; and our younger child is crying. Enough for today.

Day 3

Wow! The superintendent said that the Denver Post already reported that we were hiring Coach Stevens. I will need to get to the bottom of this issue. Coach Stevens may have thought it was an easy extra point in procuring this job. Coach Stevens has not gone through the background check nor an interview yet. There is my phone ringing and it is the Denver Post asking me when Coach Stevens starts? I asked the reporter where he obtained the information; and he replied that was from Coach Hal Stevens himself (Whoa!). The reporter then asked me about Stevens's if I was aware of the girls' track squad discrimination suit that Coach Stevens walked away from. The reporter asked if I had any other knowledge of Coach Hal Stevens discriminating while coaching. I told the reporter I was not aware of any of any further discrimination or wrongful conduct. The track squad girl athlete was appropriately demoted due to her slower times on the relay. The track athlete later stated she lied; and most probably Coach Stevens would have been exonerated within the upcoming hearings. Coach Stevens elected to move on, obtain a severance, and find another coaching job. I was not aware of any further allegations. Coach Stevens needed to still undergo a routine background check and interview. Finally, the woman reporter (who was very nice) asked about Colorado Sports Academy High School using a pro-set on offense and a 3-5 on defense. I informed her that we just are becoming organized; and, I would let her know depending on personnel.

We discussed that many skill players on offense on my recent football teams had the ability to run, catch, and throw the pigskin. On defense, I loved the 3-5 because per football rules you must have a minimum of three players on scrimmage. I also felt the 5 linebackers could shift into their power zone with some players entering the line and others following receivers in the flat. Generally, we zone with shallow and deep cover 2 or 3 depending on the opponent. The gal seemed very knowledgeable about football. She left the phone conversation saying she would be quite neutral in Coach Stevens's treatment in print. Off the record, she informed me that she lost her husband back-country skiing last year. The woman reporter inquired how I was coping with the Colorado media exploiting my widower status. All I could say is that I dearly miss Janae, I am tired, I am looking forward to the season, and there are plenty of unknowns ahead. She said she would be covering The Colorado Sports Academy High School games with the Denver Post. The gal, Missy Bradford, then asked if she could interview me, Coach Wilford Tremby. I became a bit nervous and reluctantly said yes. I have just moved here and am barely getting my feet on the ground. Most of my furniture is on a moving truck!

I hung up the phone and felt I performed adequately. I reasoned that much of this was forthcoming since I was a heavily recruited coach from Chicago. I am just a high school coach and AD; nothing more. I am worried about getting spanked by Denver 5A teams ready to crush our school off the map. I could ski right off the mountain and back to Chicago after the first football season. Fans are not of the mind-set about building a program – only immediate wins count. Losses are akin to a black mark on your soul – like a Baltimore Catechism mortal sin mark on your chest – hard to remove. I said I would never do this; but I did check out Missy Bradford on social media. Surprisingly, she is great looking, popular, and was pregnant with her first child when her former husband had the skiing accident. Again, I said I would never resort to this stuff; but here I am already showing a sliver of interest in a girl. Enough for tonight. Tuck the kids in and hope our furniture gets here tomorrow since we are tired of sleeping on floor mattresses.

Day 4

The team meeting with the parents is tonight. Everyone is anxious. Despite our team winning the Illinois state championship last year, there was no media surrounding practices or team meetings. We were unknown and just played football at Manion High School in inner city Chicago. There are many days I wish I was there and coaching football again. Sadly, I left after a 5A championship high school football run. Most people questioned the move – especially after Janae's untimely death. I told the Chicago Tribune the absolute truth about the Colorado sojourn. Chicago is over and I need to move on. I am dealing with diapers, pre-school, not having much of our personal stuff due to moving truck screw-ups. Now, I am dealing with endless school issues surrounding the team, transfer players, presumptive hire of controversial Coach Hal Stevens with an interview, and pushy parents. I am overwhelmed at night dealing with the single parent thing, Colorado Sports Academy High School expectations, lesson plans and three babies needing their mom. I will somehow get through this ordeal. Janae's parents are consumed by me being single and available. They do not understand I need some grieving time and restructuring of my emotions. I am not interested in forging into some half-baked relationship currently.

Well, the football meeting with the parents was interesting. I received a mouthful from parents, student-athletes, teachers, and administrators. Everything was discussed including my playbook, rules, grades, depth charts and of course, Hal Stevens from Denver. Many parents expressed concern having this guy in the building or on campus. I felt he needed to be given a fair shake. The superintendent then stood-up and said Stevens was implicitly and explicitly exonerated; and there were no other issues forthcoming. The Coach Stevens issue attracted a ton of conventional and social media attention in Denver – though it ended rightfully. The superintendent then said that Coach Wilford Tremby and himself would be interviewing Stevens and treating him like all the other coaching candidates. That issue was solved excepting one parent who had a frosh gal attending Colorado Sports Academy High School on the soccer team. She had grave misgivings about Stevens. I felt she was entitled to her opinion; and that she could become pro-active on the school board or PTO. She said she was attempting both.

I tucked my three little guys in on the mattress in the living room. Josh said while at kindergarten today that all moms would be coming on the field trip on Friday – the very first week of school. His new friend, Kent, down the block asked when Josh's mom would show up. I had to inform Josh again that Mom went to heaven, would not ever be back until we die, and then we would be reunited. Josh wanted to know if I was being the mom on the field trip. I said I had football practice and English class. We then stared at one another with tears in all four eyes, hugged, and I said I would be the mom on the field trip. I would advance my English class the next day's lesson and have a film session with the other coaches and players until I arrived home. We open next week against a very tough north Denver team on the road. Our football team needs to be ready.

I could not sleep now and thought about the team meeting. A dad brought up from his research that I ran a ton of RPO (run-pass options). His question was about containment of the defensive end or outside linebacker. I explained that our athletic quarterbacks would make decisions based on the immediate gap created. I love speed around the outside. Outside containment by the defense requires our flanker, tight end, and wideout to have the outside shoulder of the outside linebacker and defensive end blocked on outside defensive containment. Our QB with field vision does not necessarily have to follow the blocking

9

scheme. Our offensive line is blocking down. If we pull a tackle or guard the middle linebacker and safety will immediately follow. The QB will take the crease inside or outside if it develops. If the contain comes towards the QB, a pitch to the trail back occurs as the flanker and wideout are blocking inward. The RPO (run-pass option) also has an immediate or delayed pass option with the weak side speedy end doing a post pattern across the middle of the field. This will be open if the deep safety commits to the run. The pass must obviously lead the streaking wideout. We have got a ton of practicing ahead of us! Goodnight Janae.

Day 5

I awoke today amidst a sea of rain. These Colorado storms can be brutal; and near tornado weather occurred prompting the school district to delay classes two hours. I will get Josh to school and Jake to preschool. At least our clothes are here; and the rest of our personal belongings are arriving this afternoon. The nanny caring for Jaiden has arrived on time; and we are reviewing her salary/hours/duties. She is a UCCS student with night classes – full time three days per week. Her friend subs as nanny if I need her for evening meals and babysitting if I am gone. I found both on the internet. The kids think they have a new mom; and I am good with that. The storm appears to be receding. I am busy and will keep moving on. If I was in Chicago, my mom would have been here; and I would not be dealing with all this myself. I need to get these thoughts out of my mind.

I have a late football practice and coaches meeting. The coaches have already warned me about Coach Stevens from Denver. Further allegations have surfaced. I called the superintendent and we both decided until the allegations went through hearings, that we would defer the interview. What a relief! I feel bad for Coach Stevens; but within our society with allegations within coaching equates to guilty until proven innocent. I hope Coach Stevens gets through this mess – my research informs me he is an excellent coach of multiple sports. Thus, at the coaches meeting we will just discuss players, depth charts, offensive and defensive schemes, and prepare for the game this weekend. I want Colorado Sports Academy High School to be respectful.

I finished my lesson plans for the year and submitted them to the school board and administration for my English classes. There was some fluttering regarding the phonics, cursive, and bulletin board competitions. I explained we would all learn by having one-on-one by teams go to the blackboard and answer questions individually and through your team if needed. If Team A can get the correct adverb with proper spelling and syntax in a phrase, the team receives two points. If the team collectively gets it correct after the student is not 100%, then it is one point. If the opposition gets it correct after Team A fails, it is three points to the opposition. I am testing grammar, spelling, literature, vocabulary, phonics, proper English, and common sense. English is the global language; and it never stops expanding and yearning for us to learn common and intellectual use. Our students will know the basics and more upon finishing the year including some of the very best writers and linguistics historically – like William Shakespeare.

The field trip was great this afternoon after I hustled back to late football practice. Josh was happy as I dropped him off with our Nanny. As we left the bus, one of the apparently single recently divorced moms came upon me quite strong and asked a multitude of questions. I tried to be nice and inform her that I was not interested. She was cute and did not mind registering for a rain check. Oh my God! A single guy (now a widower) is out there waiting for a match. I want none of this now. I am not a fan of blending families since I have enough on my plate and do not need to assume another family's misgivings or life failures. Time to sign up for regular Sunday mass.

Day 6

We won the game Saturday night v a great Denver team and program. The game was fast and furious. I felt we had the better prepared players; but the ability of the opposition was perhaps a step above our team. We employed on defense a 3-5 set-up (3 down linemen and 5 linebackers). We played Cover-2 (2 deep safeties) most of the game. Their QB was dynamic and I placed our spy defensive back on the QB to follow him on sweeps, drop backs, run-pass options, or any play coming from that offense. It worked fabulously since our spy had 12 tackles and 6 on the QB. Our aim was to limit the QB and allow our air-raid offense to flourish. When we needed plays, our offense produced some great ingenuity, power, and finesse. All the drills to evade tacklers after a hand-off or pass reception worked wonderfully. I cannot be prouder of our team since we only had 2 weeks to prepare for the season opener. We now have 1 week to prepare for another Denver powerhouse. The parents, players, and school administrators were quite excited after the win. Our very first school win in any sport. Cheerleaders were incredibly excited to bring on their athleticism and energy to our team both to and from the evening football game.

Missy Bradford, the Denver Post woman reporter grabbed me before I stepped on the bus and congratulated me on a great game and plan. She twinkled at me with her eyes; and admittedly she was startling in her appearance. I thanked her and was spellbound for a moment. I jumped on the bus as the bus driver said we are leaving. The coaches all questioned me about the young reporter who was gleaming at me. I told them she came to practice a couple days out of interest for the team. Her name is Missy Bradford and she will be following our team for the Denver Post. The coaches all felt there was more than professional interest. I scoffed at these ideas and said I have plenty of issues at home. We then planned 0700 coaches meeting and film session Saturday morning for two hours; followed by a light practice with the team including light pads and film. We escaped with an ankle sprain to our punt returner; but I feel he will be ready to go in one week– our next game.

I arrived home and thanked the Nanny. I discovered that the kids really liked her; and were calling her mom. I was so tired, thanked, paid, and bonused the Nanny, and then placed the kids on now their own beds. Jayden had dirty diapers and a rash. I used Janae's special ointment and hopefully by morning it will have receded. I am on my way to bed and my text went off from Missy Bradford stating that your defensive spy on that great Denver quarterback won the game. I gave her a return thumbs-up. Reporters are graded on neutrality and fair reporting. This is not within the rules, is biased, and not even close to neutrality. I will have some future decisions to make. I am going to bed.

Day 7

The coaches meeting went well despite the nanny showing up a half hour late. I am at a crossroads with having to obtain a nanny for every step out of the house. Nannies have schedules also. Perhaps I do need a woman in my life; however, most of the women modernly are professional demanding a nanny for them. Daycare is a possibility; but daycare on weekends is expensive and tenuous. Perhaps, I just teach and not coach until these kids are older and can care for themselves. It is stressful worrying about whether the nanny will show or not show. I am at a real professional and family crossroads. I know I do not want Janae's parents here 24/7; as that would be a disaster and an opinion or ruling on everything we do here. Janae's mom would be critical of meals, hours, lifestyle, clothes and perhaps even if I went on a date. She never stops troubling myself regarding the available high-profile gals in Greenwood Village. These gals have become known to myself through social media and other avenues the Tompkins have established.

Practice with our team was tremendous. We have two full weeks to prepare for a very difficult opponent. Their skill positions, blocking, tackling and play schemes are tremendous. It will be uphill to defeat this team. We discussed surprising them with a wishbone offense and running that until they can stop the triple threats. Our QB last game with RPO (Run/Pass Option) was tremendous. We discussed the hand signal change pre-snap with the hand pointing towards our goal if scheming right and hand pointing towards our end zone if we scheme left. Attention to the contain player – be it outside linebacker or defensive end was emphasized. Players asked about sign stealing; and I said we would periodically huddle and raise our arms meaning nothing. The QB would in the huddle or with audible or hand clap signals would call the direction of the wishbone. All plays on offense would be initiated from the same backs, gaps, and schemes as our pro-set. Clapping snap counts mainly would be schemed. Barring a needed departure from our ongoing structured plays and schemes, I remain quite optimistic about maintaining integrity on both sides regarding stealing coaches sideline signs.

Josh has his first birthday party from school at 2 PM today. I will drop him off with a book present I just received on Amazon. I want to watch some early college football. I have received some very good offers from some high school and collegiate elite programs to join their staff soon. That is another move, outside of Colorado, and against Janae's wishes for our kids. I will reply due to family obligations that I cannot consider the job at present. My text rings and it is Missy Bradford asking if she can call regarding a few questions the Denver Post has regarding our team. Jake is crying and Jayden is sleeping in the back kids' car seat. Despite this, I call her back and inform her that once I pick up Josh from the birthday party and get them settled with Saturday evening meal, I will call (6 PM Ish). I am still wondering about this Missy Bradford. I think she wants a date; but it is too soon after Janae's death. Missy is a few months after her husband's skiing death; so, she is ready to move on in a relationship. I really do not want to go down this road – even though she is attractive and a good person. I need to concentrate 100% on my kids.

Day 8

I awoke on Sunday morning after staying up late with the kids playing games last evening. They had tremendous fun and slept well. Since we have received our furniture and the rooms are now all well fitted, you would think the kids would sleep in their beds. All three slept with me; and I finally fell asleep. Missy and I talked after the kids went to sleep nearly two full hours – mostly about football off the record. She explained her situation in Denver with her parents bringing her up in Highlands Ranch – near Greenwood Village. She was on a cheer team in high school and competitively cheered against Janae's team. Missy remembered her well because they were both captains. The cheerleading state competition was in the Denver Coliseum with those two teams fighting for the state championship. Interesting, their families knew each other additionally through social connections. I nearly asked her for a date; but then came to my senses because I am just not ready. Missy asked if she could attend a couple practice sessions. I warned against any recording devices and she agreed.

Sherry and Herb Tompkins arrived at our house Sunday at 4 PM with a basket of food and presents for the kids. We talked about the job, schools, and daycare for the kids. Sherry Tompkins inquired about my love life. I under-reacted to Janae's Mom and said I was not ready. This was somewhat upsetting to Janae's parents as they cannot possibly understand how I can cope with the child duties, coaching, and teaching responsibilities. I informed them that I appreciated their sincere interest in my wellbeing; but the dating and personal stuff would be on my own per Janae's directives. The Tompkins grumbled and moved on. I let them know that Janae knew her parents would be intimately interested in my private life.

I certainly appreciate their family interest; but it is difficult and uphill to inform relatives that you are just not ready for a relationship.

After they left about 1900 hours the kids laying on our bed repeatedly stated they wanted a brand-new puppy – just born. I said with reluctance that we would seriously consider a family pet puppy. The neighbors down the street had a cocker-spaniel baby and were quite happy. The puppy was house-broke in two weeks. I feel the kids without a mom deserve a puppy – though I know I will be the caretaker and master. I will deal with the issues as long as the kids remain happy. I will scout out the litter; and hopefully they still had a baby puppy not sold.

My assistant coach as offensive coordinator called late Sunday evening with concerns over the wishbone. He felt the offense was too predictable and without a consistent passing attack. I explained for our team to beat a powerhouse, we had to control (hog) the ball, not allow their offense on the field, and our only hope of winning was to keep it close until the end. He understood as we added a passing wrinkle over the phone. I also added a double reverse to keep the defense honest – making that play in the first quarter. I love football!

Day 9

School has been very busy with my English, phonics, and literature classes. I have full classes and have been asked to add more students and classes – though my schedule is stuffed this semester. I enjoy teaching along with coaching. All my classes begin with basic spelling, phonics, cursive writing (no computers in many classes), and literature. I feel all our students need to be aware of all the great writers, emulate these masters, and begin to create grammatically correct writings. Our classes delve into music with Renaissance and post Renaissance writings and music. The father of the Baroque period was Johann Sebastian Bach – who wrote, performed, and instructed classical music with the addition of appoggiaturas, trills, embellishments, and poignant resolving dissonance throughout his pieces. It would require a student to play 60 years 24/7 non-stop to capture all that Bach wrote. Culturally, all of today's music of many genres emanate from Bach. I studied music for many years. Many parents wanted myself to instruct piano; but the music department is just down the hall. Perhaps after coaching is music instruction.

Writing takes many forms in the English language – be it a novel, short story, musical or theatrical script play, letter, email, book report, journalism, or text message. I want our students to be educated and master the basics of English and literature. I sent home a homework assignment on Stephen Sondheim, the Father of American Broadway. After lecturing the students about his musicals and written and performed classic Broadway tunes, I wanted them all to bring a piece of Sondheim to class tomorrow. I led by informing the class that Sondheim was nearly abandoned at age 10, grew up with Oscar Hammerstein II, and wrote the music for 16 Broadway musicals such as West Side Story, Sweeney Todd, and many others in collaboration with the very best writers on Broadway. I wanted the class to expand on the genius of Sondheim by bringing one fact about Sondheim to class. My pearl is that he played the 16 Bach Invention pieces daily.

Tomorrow is puppy day. I am prepared; and the kids are so excited. Football practice is intensifying with many players becoming far better than expected. I feel we can compete. Good night!

Day 10

Life can be tumultuous teaching in high school modernly due to social media, parental, and administrative pressure. Working as a high school teacher, you become a mini-celebrity. As a coach, you become the icon if you win; and the toilet if you lose. If you are 500 and win half your games, you are unmistakably mediocre and need to be replaced. I have a new school with new athletes and expectations. I do not feel my guys on the football team are anything close presently to my Chicago championship 5A team from last year. My job is to get them there – at the premier of their potential. Unfortunately, this is not easy with variable work ethics, parents, high academic standards at our new school (Colorado Sports Academy High School) and other distractions. My main theme has been to keep practices at a reasonable length and focus on improvements in times and efficiencies. If the wheel route is not completed without defense on 10 out of 10 throws, we start a new sequence. I want my players prepared for competition between and among themselves. Weekly, we are having NFL combine drills with strength and conditioning, pass routes, tires, special forces drills – the works. Some players and even coaches complain by their actions; but I need to go beyond the limits and develop a winning attitude and culture through a hard work ethic. A missed routine tackle could mean the game and potentially playoffs.

I am adopting an old wishbone set to confuse Colorado High School football. Few teams coach and most cannot defend the QB runs, pitches, off tackle hand-offs, and passes – truly offensive options. Most passes will emanate from our pro-set. The pro-set has a single I-back, flanker, two wideouts, and tight end. If the tight end is not lined up against a defender, I will pull an audible directing the tight end to slant inward or outward depending on the opposing linebacker. If open I will have an immediate pass thrown to him off the line of scrimmage. Otherwise, I will pull him back into the pocket for pass protection – an unusual blocker for the QB pocket protection. Confusing the defense, I will utilize in the 4th quarter a tackle eligible – which, if successful, brings enormous complaints from the opposition. My standard is to inform the refs, maintain the tackle eligible with a number between 50 and 79, and line him up as a tight end. It works generally in the 4th quarter because nobody is expecting the pass play to an offensive tackle. When I am third and short, I will shoot the tackle eligible in the flat with linebackers crashing and defensive backs worrying about fake runs and deep threats. Our tackle eligible must be able to catch with gloves on; and endless practice for the one or two plays per game is needed. Occasionally, I will pull the stunt in the first quarter. Tackle eligible is an amazing part of football lore; and catches very good defensive teams off-guard.

Josh woke up this morning on the weekend and had already scouted out the neighbor's cocker spaniel pups. They were all sold within 48 hours; but one male was returned last night. He is pulling at my shirt to travel down the block as a family and purchase this puppy. It is 0530; and a phone call would be appropriate. I need to discover the pup owner's phone number; and besides, Jake and Jaiden are still sleeping in their bunks. I then informed Josh I was walking around the block for stretching. I walked out the back door and headed towards the neighbor who has the pup (who I do not know). I will just guess that he is house breaking the new pup and is outside. I find him outside coercing the new baby cocker spaniel to pee; we introduce ourselves and he already knows Josh (playing outside in the backyard). The neighbor, Thomas Whitten, informs me that the owner returned the pup without any reason and did not want his money back. The pup is worth $400 or more; but he states he will donate to a new owner so he can get his life back to normal. I said we were in the business of finding a new puppy; and immediately he offered the cocker spaniel pup with papers as a freebie. I offered to pay; but he said win some games and we are flush. I thought there is now neighborhood pressure to win.

I carried the pup back home and walked in the door as all three boys were waiting. I informed my kids I found this little guy down the street needing a home. They fell in love and poured some milk in a large bowl of which it required 30 seconds for the pup to drink. I said we need a name for this guy (he was a male). Josh and Jaiden said Spark; so, it is Spark. We need a dog bed, leash, blanky – the works. My day is at the pet store or Amazon. I am now a superhero in my own house. Janae would think I have done the right thing. I realized my kids are far more important than my English teaching job or coaching. Again, Janae is looking down thinking I have done the best I could without her. I cry a touch wishing Janae could be here with me to relish the moment with our kids.

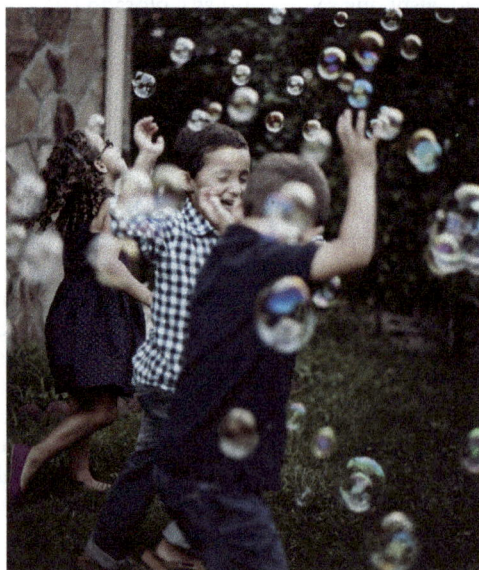

16

Day 11

Today was a crazy day for myself. I am struggling to keep my diary continuing – always thinking of Janae wanting me to record our family for our future kids, grandkids, and other family members. Diaries are mainly for females; but now I am starting to think this was a great idea of Janae's. I sit up and night and try to read after my diary is completed. Some nights I honestly cannot sleep; but that is expected after losing my beloved wife. Janae's not coming back; and I will grieve the rest of my life to a degree. I need to move on, not be depressed, and involve myself with meaningful relationships. It does not help having Janae's parents upstream in Greenwood Village. In time, they will have to accept me and my family with life matters. Sherry, Janae's mom, never stops wanting to "line me up" with a wealthy reputable family's daughter. I have implicitly and explicitly said I was not ready; and perhaps could develop relationships by myself. I am far more concerned about my three kids, teaching, and coaching job at Colorado Sports Academy High School. At present, I do not have time for a relationship with a gal; but in time perhaps I will develop a partnership. I need to keep moving on.

My English students are the very best. We are studying basic grammar on an expedited scale. Students and athletes are transferring to Colorado Sports Academy High School with varied backgrounds. I want 100% of our students learning basic English, learning to write (Including cursive), and develop practical use of phonics. These are "old school" courses which prepare students for life skills. Despite computers which can be programmed to do anything, computers cannot reason like humans. Written prose captures moods, feelings, and the tenor of the writer and the subject. I want to inspire our students who attend our class to be totally prepared for college and life. My lessons in literature, phonics, English, and written prose are intended to last a lifetime. I expect our students to publish, write books, communicate with articulation, and enjoy life. I set my pen down and I receive a text from Missy Bradford who wants to talk. I call her back and she wants to attend football practice tomorrow since the game Friday night is receiving tons of media attention. I texted back and said she could attend practice with no phone on or video equipment. I've also need to be prepared to attend Josh's parent – teacher night tomorrow. The back-up nanny is coming; and I am looking forward to meeting with Josh's teacher. He is doing well in kindergarten. Spark, our baby puppy, is barking and needs to attend to his bathroom duties outside. Tomorrow is a big day!

Day 12

What a day! Practice was great because our team hit the blocking sleds with motivation and spirit. These guys want to win football games. I can handle a loss if our team gives 110%. I feel we are now focused and I have stressed our peck order of God/family as #1, academics #2, and football #3. These guys need support from all angles including the administration, teachers, coaches, fans, and media. Normally, I am not a fan of having media at practice; but Missy Bradford from the Denver Post has been quite helpful and positive in her coverage of Colorado Sports Academy High School. Her articles discuss our approach, strategy, training, and she has been quite upbeat and thoughtful covering our coaches. People know I coached an inner-city Chicago High School football team to the state championship. I plan on completing the same task in Colorado. I am finally impressed that our team is jelling because we have a tough opponent Friday night in Denver. Our QB has caught fire with his run-pass options and overall field and situational awareness while playing. He has made some great QB runs which have turned the tide in our first two games we won. We have utilized conventional and non-conventional defenses to confuse the opposition. Our turnover margins are positive; so, our instructions over ball security are succeeding.

I received a call from Janae's Mom about an afternoon social at her house in Greenwood Village. I am certain Sherry Tompkins (Janae's mom) wants me to meet an eligible family friend's daughter. This will not ever stop; and I will just have to deal with Janae's parents. Perhaps I should not have moved here while trying to admonish Janae's desires to have our kids raised on the front range of Colorado rather than inner city Chicago. I want to get along with Janae's parents; and her mom will never stop until I have a replacement mom. I have told her repeatedly I am not ready for a relationship; and her response has been that I need to be involved in a relationship, marry, and live happily ever after. Thus, if attend this Sunday afternoon social, I will need to dress up (not my favorite for Sunday afternoon), hire the nanny for more weekend coverage, and deal with asking for a date with someone I do not know. Alternatively, I will have to deal with Janae's parents if I do not respectfully ask this eligible person for a dinner date. I do not have time for any of this with three little kids. I need to think this matter through.

I received a call from one of assistant coaches just before falling asleep. He informs me that most of our offensive line has influenza, will not be at practice the rest of the week, and the docs are informing them to bag this weekend's game. I am frozen because our replacements are a big drop in ability, maturity, size, and overall game. We cannot afford false starts, off-sides, holding, or any other mishaps. I will talk to the parents and docs tomorrow morning and we will formulate a plan of attack. I realized illness and injuries are part of the competitive game, and our team and coaches will just deal with the issues and situation. Initially, I thought I would inform Missy Bradford (the Denver newspaper sports reporter following our team). The more I contemplate the situation, I will need to adjust and perhaps say our second-string line is "stepping up" if I am asked. I will deal!

Day 13

Love is the very last thought on my mind. I am struggling with my job, the kids, coaching, and impediments emotionally and physically. I have started to jog (a millennial sport). I think a ton when I jog – especially about my football team, the loss of my wife (Janae), our kids, and whether I need to delve into the "singles" market. I feel I am still grieving over Janae (it has been 3 months from her death from metastatic (everywhere) breast cancer). I cry at night with many nights my body receiving minimal sleep. This is total grief; and it seems I will never get through this. A new female relationship may guide me through this grief; but then again, I will end up in a funnel into marriage relationship. There are obvious risks to any relationship. I do not want to attend to a gal; and then risk one of us "dumping" the supposed partner. I need to get over this thought. Janae has passed; and I need a new life. Perhaps I need to move back to Chicago. This idea is moving backwards because Janae wanted our kids to be mountain Coloradoans as youth. Janae wanted these kids skiing, playing hockey, snowshoeing, throwing snowballs, ice fishing, and cycling on mountain trails. That sounds great; but it seems my stress level was less because the teaching and coaching in inner city Chicago had few expectations. There was no football legacy at Manion High School in Chicago; but I created a monster with ever-increasing crowds, student body support, and Chicago media exploding with coverage for our high school championship 5A team. We loved it! Nobody knows and respects that in Colorado. Instead, I have received a startup venture (Colorado Sports Academy High School) with parents dreaming of Olympic gold. We have won two close football games by the seat of our pants.

I arrived home and Sherry Tompkins (Janae's mom) had dismissed and paid the nanny. Janae's parents (Sherry and Herb Tompkins) have a house key. Sherry was helping Josh with his kindergarten homework of numbers, letters, and early spelling. I loved this scene. Sherry was cool; and after she made supper and settled the kids into bed with nighttime stories. Sherry proposed that I arrive on time and dress appropriately for her social Sunday afternoon in Greenfield Village. She admitted there would be eligible young attractive women who would fit what I needed. All Greenfield Village knows of my situation; and there are plenty of young women of means willing to step into Janae's shoes. Sherry said she realized they would never be a biological mom; but it would be the very best thing for our family if I settled, married, and had a life-long partner. Sherry then discussed Missy Bradford, and knew she was "flirting" with me. I informed Sherry Tompkins that nothing has occurred and may never occur. Sherry then explained that it was important that my next partner or spouse be from the correct family. This would be an upgrade from Missy Bradford's family roots. I was shocked, but under-reacted. Moving to Colorado I expected a little from the Tompkins as Janae's parents with nearness to me regarding the "girl" thing. I never expected the immense pressure mounting on this formal Sunday afternoon greeting party where I am supposed to meet, request a date, and ultimately connect lifelong with an eligible mate in Greenfield Village. Sherry tucked the three grandkids into bed and left accomplishing her mission. I need a cold Coors beer.

Day 14

I awoke the next morning early and arrived at a thought of playing with nine men on the line offensively for the upcoming game. My offensive line is still virus ridden; and will not be playing on Friday night in Denver. I have received calls from Missy Bradford (the Denver sports reporter) asking questions about the team strength with the upcoming duel in Denver under the lights. I was reserved and felt that giving away any ammunition to the press and subsequently to the Denver reigning champs of our league would be disaster. Our subs have begun to surface and play quite well. I am altering our attack with one tailback, the ends not so split, and the line double teaming everywhere they can for both passing and running. Some of the pass plays will have one eligible receiver downfield. The QB will have run-pass options continuously through the evening; and understands his role as a "gamer." The assistant coaches have firmed the defense with only a couple starters potentially missing some or all the game. The replacement defensive subs are quite good and "game ready." The team is hungry and wants to prove they belong. I am loving the attitude of this youthful team. The grades on our football team are superb excepting our great punter. The punter has been "talked to" by our assistant coaches and a tutor was readied. This has helped the punter's grade situation immensely. All our footballers know how I feel about grades. There is no football without the best grades they can produce. I want 110% in the classroom and field.

I ran early this morning – covering 7 miles in a little over an hour. I passed Spark's (our cocker-spaniel) original home. I noticed the philanthropic owner (nickname Smitty) working out in the backyard and he waved at me and came running. Smitty thanked me for our kid's friendship and I thanked him for the puppy. We talked openly; and he admitted he was just coming around after a tumultuous relationship with his former wife. Smitty's former wife suffered from addiction and refused treatment. She needed to be hospitalized and eventually placed in an institution with a diagnosis of bipolar schizophrenia that developed shortly after their three kids were born. Smitty was a highly successful IT engineer; and very intelligent. We both talked openly; and he said he would not be on the planet if he had not enlisted an on-line life coach. Smitty's catharsis on life was compelling. Smitty moved on from a disastrous family situation. The entire neighborhood knew my situation; and I was a topic of discussion over the neighborhood fences. I admitted being ambivalent about relationships so early after Janae's early death. I jogged home and got the kids ready for the nanny and school. Perhaps I do need a life coach to ease my transition as a widower. Smitty gave me the name of his life coach – whom he periodically reconnects. I will think on this one because we have got an upcoming big game in Denver this week. A life coach…hmmm…interesting.

Day 15

We prepared well with second string linemen and won the football game on a fumbled 2-point extra point attempt after the favored Denver school drove 80 yards in the last 3 minutes to get within a point of our school, Colorado Sports Academy. The game was crowded and I was quite happy with our team excepting the last drive because they kept converting 3rd and 4th downs on the last-minute offensive drive. I intended to stop this team with everything in our defensive playbook but we could not develop a plan of blitzing, zone defense by rushing three linemen (the rule minimum on scrimmage) with an 8-man zone. We lost outside contain on three occasions which resulted in first down with substantial gains. I was upset with myself and the fumble bailed our team out with a bad snap that we recovered on the one-yard line. I somewhat felt sorrow for the opposition because I have been on the other side when we call a play that works

20

99% in practice – yet game emotions enter just a simple snap or hand-off. Football is a funny sport because it excites us all with its pageantry, gladiator mentality, and the nuances of offense/defense/special teams. Football is such a big part of my life; but also highly interested in English/phonics/literature instruction – my true love. Eventually, I want to teach music part-time; after the kids are gone. Janae loved music – perhaps it is time for Josh to begin piano lessons. He has got a lot on his plate with the neighborhood soccer team, kindergarten all-day, and just playing with his friends on the block – like Smitty's kids.

Smitty's catharsis on life with his on-line coach made me think I need to contact his life coach. The coach's name is Sandy Swift. She is from Seattle; and runs a professional service for a reasonable price. Sandy is a trained psychologist who does not believe in psychiatric meds – barring severe mental disease. Her counseling redirects the mind into a positive frame – allowing difficult decisions to be straightforward and sensible. I believe I need that advice because I am confused regarding dating, in-laws at Greenfield Village in Denver, and my role as a coach and teacher at Colorado Sports Academy. The biggest part of me that needs help is my grief. I need to move on; but I still see Janae daily, talk to her while taking a shower, and occasionally cry. The kids still feel Mom's returning; but eventually they will understand about breast cancer.

Missy Bradford called and wanted to know if I wanted to attend a block party in Castle Rock at one of the former Bronco's home Sunday afternoon. I did not know what to say because that is a date – though informal. I told her I would get back to her asap because I need to check my kids' schedules. I feel it is too early to date; but I like Missy Bradford. Once I plunge into a relationship, it is on a serious tract towards you know what (marriage). I will call Sandy Swift tomorrow and do a Skype life coach relationship. I just do not know about dating.

Day 16

On the very first life coach encounter I was quite pleased. Sandy Swift said I had a few issues to resolve. Grief is still highly present and can linger and destroy one's life. The life-coach highly mentioned to essentially place Janae into a celebration of life context, be happy we had the time together, and move-on. I discussed the Missy Bradford date and block party. Sandy, the life coach, mentioned that if the setting is right for a relationship, then take it. The next relationship may be years – if ever. The relationship with Missy Bradford may be friends, girlfriends,

21

or something more. Remember, she has issues of grief and moving on from her husband's death. Missy may have issues with a relationship with a guy that has three young kids and her being a de-facto Mom. The on-line coach (Sandy Swift) was wonderful in helping me deal with my in-laws, Sherry and Herb Tompkins. Thus, I need to inform the Tompkins that despite me having a great time at the Sunday party last week, I had no immediate interest in any of the available single gals present. That may upset them, but it is also my life. I am not marrying Janae's parents. I do appreciate their strong interest in being good grandparents. I feel the Tompkins pushing me into a relationship is their way of dealing with Janae's death and moving on. I am more comfortable discussing this with them openly now.

Our Saturday coaches meeting was superb. New plays, redesigns of the wishbone and pro-sets on offense were completed with more misdirect against advancing teams with real team speed. Colorado Sports Academy has an uphill fight against the football powerhouses; but we are holding our own on offense, defense, and special teams. The defensive coaches have added a new wrinkle with a free safety blitz on one side; while the corner blitzes on the other side. Our linebackers have been replaced with backup defensive backs for pass coverage on these special defensive schemes. We are at risk for runs; but when it is 2nd or 3rd and long, we are going with the opposite defensive back blitzes to confuse the offense. The opposition has seen film of us and already planned their playbook opposing our strengths when we ultimately meet and play.

I am quite happy with the early parent-teacher conferences and how the parents have responded to the phonics, fundamental English, and literature presenta-tions. I want my students reading and learning. Students are wanting to transfer into our classes; but I am full and stuffing the classroom makes life difficult for the rest of the students and myself. I am honored that I am in demand; and it makes me quite happy that the students are virtually all thinking college with humanity studies as part of their curriculum. Tucking in the kids with reading "A Cat in the Hat" for Josh, Jake, and Jayden resulted in all three falling asleep in their bunks. I love it!

Day 17

The kids all came down with red cheeks today; and all had runny nose, slight cough, low grade fever, and congestion. I obtained a pediatric appointment early and was not late for my English class. The pediatrician (Alison Maples DO) was compassionate, knowledgeable, and cute. I noticed from wall plaques that she obtained her medical school in Kirksville. Missouri; and residency at Iowa City. She just started with a small pediatric group and had very athletic pictures of her cycling, skiing, running, and swimming about her office. I asked her about the pictures and she said prior to residency (a killer), she was a gal jock. Now she just works out at Lifetime Fitness, skis, and cycles on weekends, and occasionally does the triathlon circuit. Dr. Maples reviewed our charts and mentioned under family history that since Janae died from early breast cancer, our kids may be at risk for cancer genes. In time, that will need to be evaluated with blood and genetic testing. Dr. Alison Maples then asked me how I was doing/coping with the loss of Mom. I retorted that I had misgivings about moving to Colorado; but I am intent on making it work. I noticed no wedding or engagement ring on her finger; and she smiled at me a ton. She diagnosed the kids with 5th disease with the slapped cheek appearance, gave me an education sheet, and will see all three kids in a week. Tylenol, liquids, and home school was prescribed.

As I was rescheduling with the young noisy front office scheduler, Harper Smith, she mentioned she was following our team (Colorado Sports Academy High School). Harper's boyfriend had read my book on quarterbacking; and she loved the Broncos. And Harper mentioned with a smile that Dr. Maples liked me. I walked out with my three young guys wondering what all that meant. What is like? Like in the English language can be a noun, preposition, conjunction, adjective, or adverb -depending on how it is applied – meaning the context of the speech. Thus, being liked could mean similar characteristics, similar ways, reference, a meaningless filter, or to convey an attitude. Like could mean our family is normal, not unprofessional like many patients are, or fondness – like a girl liking or having a crush on a guy. Why did Harper Smith at the front office inform me of this so quickly. I now must return in a week to the same front office and physician who "likes" me. It is embarrassing! I can be cool; deal with this gorgeous professional; and get these kids through 5th disease. I am thinking this is how I met Janae – serendipity. Dr. Maples being seen at football practice like Janae? No way! Onto school.

Day 18

We experienced an intense coach's meeting today after practice. We have a couple linebackers with grade issues. Thus, we are bringing in their parents and discussing the situation. Both players need to advance and improve their grades; or, they are not playing or practicing football (the rule). I am insistent that all players obtain a minimum of a B average. We are undefeated entering our 4th game at home against a tough Colorado Springs opponent. Our opponent has a strong legacy of winning football, places a few players in all college divisions yearly, and has a stubborn head coach. I feel we are well prepared, in game shape and we are now ranked 7th in Class 5A within the state of Colorado. I could not be happier. We are favored in the Friday night contest; but I feel any wrong bounce of the football could lead to a close loss. All our team can do is play hard and strive to win the game.

My life coach, Sandy Swift, was quite good and knowledgeable about my situation. I told her about our kids' pediatrician. The life coach mentioned that relationships blossom unexpectedly; and can occur at any moment. She did mention the Berlin Wall code between doctors and patients; and if anything happened beyond friendship, that we would be required to find another kiddy doctor. I am perplexed by all of this; but feel perhaps I need to start dating. My life coach feels it is acceptable and a manner of dealing with grief, unhappiness, and a need to have relationships beyond acquaintances. This was a great session; and I feel I have a log laying on my brain removed.

I saw Smitty down the block while jogging early today. We discussed the life coach and the pediatrician. Smitty's advice was to take it slow, weave into a relationship, and let things naturally happen. Smitty asked if I had checked out the pediatrician on social media. I had not dug into that aspect of her life; and besides, all I know is that the front desk person liked football and said the pediatrician liked me. Smitty had already drawn up a Tik-Tok account of her; and she moved to Colorado from Des Moines after being dumped by a real estate guy. Smitty said, "There you go. She is available!" I am spell bound; and forgot that Missy Bradford wanted me to attend a former Bronco player's house party Sunday afternoon. Smitty laughed as we discussed the situation – replying it is better to have two than zero. I am befuddled. I need to get breakfast going for the kids.

Day 19

We won the game Friday night on a late field goal kick that hit the upright and fell through. Our team was extraordinarily happy because we are undefeated at 4 games into the season and now ranked #3. The Denver newspaper with Missy Bradford covering us has highlighted our team players and coaching staff. The school (Colorado Sports Academy High School) has been highlighted as an academic yet sports school. They have placed me as a professor with rock hard English and Literature classes; and one who still teaches cursive and phonics. We have now had many more parents and students wanting to attend our school; and my classes are stuffed. Missy Bradford called about the former Denver Bronco player party she wanted me to attend. Missy's coverage was so incredibly great that I said yes. I do not know if this is a date or a gathering? I will find out and just enjoy the day (tomorrow). Our coaches meeting went well; and our assistant coaches are on high ground with many wanting a state championship. I said one play at a time on special teams, offense, or defense. We worked on special cover 3 defensive zone defense on the blackboard. The division of 1/3 in the defensive backfield would depend on where the opposition receiver's line up. We mimic man-to-man defense by lining up against the receivers when they come to the line of scrimmage. Suddenly, when cadence begins, we snap into zone coverage confusing the quarterback and receivers. Occasionally, we stay with man pass receiving defense creating more confusion. I love it! We discussed on offense getting our speed receivers the ball in the flats in space to overcome slower linebackers and defensive backs. Our snap counts were being anticipated by some defenses. We placed a color within the cadence to confuse the defense (it means nothing and our audibles remain the same).

Herb and Sherry Tompkins came down to babysit for the kids while I was at the coaches' meetings. Sherry again inquired about my love life and if I had any relationships. My life coach, Sandy Swift – Nurse Practitioner, advised me to confront the Tompkins on this issue, and allow them to understand that I need to live my personal life within myself (it is not public). Thus, I told Sherry and Herb Tompkins that I had a date tomorrow in Denver with Missy Bradford. They read her sports columns daily; and like the press coverage. The Tompkins neighborhood is quite excited about our team; as is Smitty and the neighborhood within our immediate housing area. I also told the Tompkins about Alison Maples DO pediatrician. That woke them up! Sherry just assumed I would be chasing the doctor! I informed her that the office secretary informed me that the pediatrician liked me as we were leaving. And I again informed Janae's parents that could mean we were good patients comparably, we were friendly, she was getting paid for her services, or perhaps she really did like me as in wanting a relationship. That aroused the Tompkins; but I assured them that there is a Berlin Wall between doctor and patient. That is no different than myself knowing a wall exists between my students and staff peers and myself as a teacher. You do not go there. Sherry insisted that there was something there, and I need to follow up. It is undeniable that Sherry wants involvement in her grandkids potential next stepmom. At least I had the guts through my life coach to discuss openly what was happening to my personal life. I need to hit the bed after bedtime stories for Josh, Jake, and Jayden.

Day 20

The date with Missy Bradford went well. I talked to many other coaches and players who took note of Colorado Sports Academy High School's football program this year. Many were asking about the pro and wishbone set on offense, the reverse on kickoff returns, and our blitz packages. The food was Mexican; and it was scrumptious. Missy appeared great; and was unmistakably beautiful with her blonde hair and eloquent dress. I met many VIPs from Denver, some of the Broncos since they had a bye this week, and some political people. Many people knew I had coached our Chicago team (Manion High School) to a 5A championship. It was a beautiful home in Highlands Ranch – not far from my home in Monument, Colorado. I was invited to some Bronco games, other future parties, and a poker night. I honestly appreciated all the offers but admittedly have little kids that demand 99% of my attention when not teaching or coaching. Everyone seemed to know my situation. Missy was extremely comforting and was honest regarding her situation as a widow; and understood I needed time before any relationship would occur. We parted with a kiss; and it felt good. I honestly do not know what to do next if anything.

Josh, Jake, and Jayden are all active with our puppy, Spark. We walk the puppy together; and he was easy to house train. We walked by Smitty's house and the kids played while I held the puppy on a leash. Smitty was his usual bright self in explaining life's issues. Smitty always comes to a resolution; and his experience says a ton. He wanted to know details of the Denver Bronco party, if anything was going on with Alison Maples DO pediatrician, and what I am doing with the Colorado social media popularity as a winning coach. I mentioned that no serious relationships were occurring; and our team was winning close games through conditioning and fundamentals. Smitty loved all this talk. He said I was in a good position; and to stay afloat without a "rushed" relationship. We discussed potentially having a beer together after the kids went down tomorrow night. I felt it was a great idea; and I would determine where I was after the kids retired into bed post bedtime stories – they are now addicted to stories and books.

Josh was asked to go skiing when the slopes opened by a friend and fellow classmate down the block. We have zero ski equipment; but per Janae, I am not standing in the way of our kids enjoying Colorado slopes. We are attending an early season ski swap after practice tomorrow night. Both of us will obtain equipment and hit the slopes. The phone rang late and I thought it was a scam call. Surprisingly, it was Alison Maples DO who wanted to know how the kids were doing. After we settled their improvements from 5th Disease (the slapped face red cheeks and fever are gone), she started talking about social stuff and how she just moved here. She inquired about myself and we talked for a half hour freely. The pediatrician talked about her difficult cases, medical politics, moving here from Omaha after a difficult relationship, and adjusting to Colorado. Alison Maples DO can ski as she has incurred many ski trips living in Omaha, Nebraska. I mentioned that our kids were asked to ski (well just Josh). The pediatrician said she could instruct. Oh my God! The like that her medical secretary informed me was a like towards a relationship. Smitty was right (I am 2-0). The bases are loaded and now I am up to bat. Oh my God! She is cute! What am I to do?

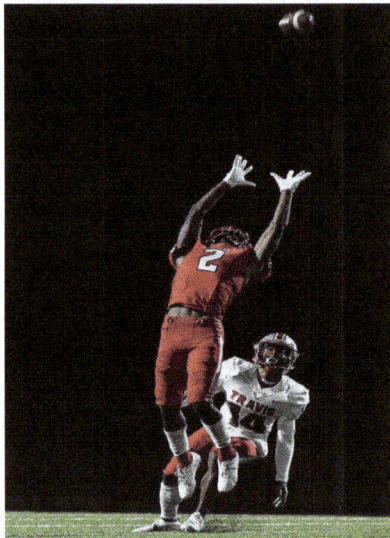

Day 21

The English class today was heartwarming. After a lengthy discussion of personal pronouns and the direct and indirect objects of pronouns within writing skills, a sophomore student presented a writing that won 2nd in the National Scholastic writing contest for high school. The reviewers loved the writing and made a couple critical comments on the careful use of her pronouns having a clear antecedent (referring to the noun which relates to the later pronoun). This can cause confusion when there is more than one noun or subject potentially relating to the pronoun. We discussed this in class; and I said I wanted clarity with all our writings – despite seemingly being not obviously duplicative. The reader must exactly know who or what is being referred to when writing. Short simple understandable sentence structure within the writing makes for a great treatise. Depending on the context and form of writing, I want our students to get to the point, express themselves clearly, and not pivot the reader in varying directions.

We emphasize the second semester would be a culmination of everyone in the class writing a short story – my favorite form of prose. The characters, setting, theme, plot, and conclusions would all be stated upfront in their proposal. I would help them achieve a formal published short story writing.

Smitty came over after the kids went to bed for a Thursday night beer and watching Thursday night football. Smitty is a real football fan; and I have received a few ideas from his mind regarding misdirect plays on offense and masquerading blitzes on defense. Smitty feels that winning requires preparation, execution, and planning to catch your opponents off guard. Obtaining a 10-yard sac on a critical drive places the offense under stress and allows the defense to build in plenty of safeguards (like an extra defensive back). We laughed and said with the potential new electronic first downs, there would still be controversy when and where a knee or elbow touched. There would still be some controversy where the ball was in relationship to the electronic stop. All the reviews with slow motion and multiple views the ball placement remains not exactly discernable. Instant replay is confusing to the booth reviewers. Both Smitty and I are taking the call on the field and living with the results (good or bad). The human element in officiating with the speed involved has eclipsed instant replay in many cases. Both of us feel depending on the game score and where the ball is on the field, more 4th down attempts in lieu of punting should occur. Smitty was getting ready to leave when the phone rang on speaker. It was Missy Bradford wanting to watch practice tomorrow. I replied yes if no recordings are completed. Smitty laughed as he walked out the door as Missy wanted to talk further. Missy Bradford is obviously interested in me. I need to decide soon. A life coach session is upcoming.

Day 22

The Friday practice went well in preparation for our upcoming Homecoming game Saturday afternoon. I pulled our team off the field after some difficult 90-minute drills. We had three offensive strings march up and down the field with 7 skill players. The cadence and coming off the line of scrimmage timely with immediate assignments was relentless. I wanted our guys to understand and know the wishbone offense subconsciously. If a substitute entered the game, there was no diminution of play. The wishbone is entirely dependent on every player knowing their position well and executing the offense. Missy Bradford was there and in return for her invite I graciously invited her over to our house after practice. Our kids were finishing school and wanted to play with Smitty's and other neighbors' kids. They play this game derived from a Wisconsin bred neighbor called the "Keen Game." The kids divide by picking 2 teams based on speed. There is a defensive team (guards the goal) and a scoring offensive team with a home house as the goal. The porch or perhaps the garage is designated as the scoring goal which the hiding scoring team must touch before they are touched by the defense. Both teams meet at the goal and then the scoring team hides in the neighborhood over a 60 count. The hiding offensive team then tries to sneak to the goal without being noticed. If they are visualized, any member of the defensive team can knock them out by touching them before they touch the goal. There are maddening rushes to the goal or designated house. If all the scoring team members touch the goal, they get to be on offense again. The game continues until darkness; however, our kids play until past dark with pleadings. We have ice cream at one of the neighbor's houses; and tonight, the ice cream treat is at our house. I am ready with lots of different flavored ice cream.

Missy finished the article for the Denver newspaper; and then wanted to talk about relationships. I was totally caught off-guard. Since I am a typical male and am quiet about such matters, I let her lead the discussion. I felt we should take our time and just get to know one another. This was barely okay for Missy or any serious girl to hear. I did not know what to say since I am still grieving over Janae. My life coach has encouraged me to move on. The Nurse Practitioner coach on line mentioned that if a relationship felt good; then potentially "go for it!" I do not know if I am there yet; but I am working on it. The kids returned and we had 15 sitting around the table eating ice cream. My son, Josh, who is a talkative kid, told the rest of the kids that Missy was probably our new "mom." Missy smiled and said we are not there yet. Again, I did not know what to say. I am getting in over my head; and this is a life coach and Smitty discussion. The homecoming football game is enough for me to swallow. I need to focus. I walked the kids home with Missy because it was dark. We fist pumped our parting. That was cool. I got an online session with the life coach, Sandy, tomorrow morning at 0600. There are gobs of issues to discuss.

Day 23

There are subliminal issues ongoing with me that my mental health nurse practitioner life coach, Sandy Swift FNP, wants me to work on. She mentioned many women will push the envelope into a relationship without me realizing where I am at; and then chart the future course. Obviously, the intent is to remarry with these serious dates if it works. As a coach and guy, it is not that I am backing away from a woman relationship; it is that I have three young kids and need to care for them. Everyone thinks I need a wife; and if that happens – great. I hear that in my classroom, teachers' lounge and on the football field. Janae's parents feel I am treading water with many good eligible women wanting to potentially adopt kids and have more. It is almost too much for me to handle. I do need some socialization outside of my family, school, and football. There's very little time; and I have got constant nanny issues. The Tompkins have been quite good in babysitting when I run short of a nanny. I am needing a nanny for many years to come; and the one that I have is quite good (Mandy). Her backup (Aiden) is quite good also. Both are college students and they will be gone in time. I will worry about that when that time occurs.

The coaches arrived Thursday night for a brief coaches' meeting at my house. We performed some film study on our Colorado Springs opponent for Homecoming. We elected to use both the pro set with 2 backs and the wishbone by altering backs and quarterbacks. Both QBs are ready for the challenge. I want to confuse the defense because they are one of the top defenses. The only way we can score is to outcoach them. The opponent plays a 5-2 defense – respecting our passing game. That is where I feel we can make progress with options, misdirect plays, and jet sweeps – since our timing has been excellent with endless practice reps.

The kids were at Smitty's house during the coaches' meeting. Jayden came home in our wagon crying with dirty diapers. Josh stayed to play the evening keen game and Jake had some homework to finish. I helped him with the homework – easy math. Josh and Jake are doing well in school. They inform their friends that they are getting a new mom. That is even more pressure. Josh came home after I tucked in the younger two boys with a black eye. I am having a beer before retiring and thinking about the game more than ever. It will be a close contest. We have a flea-flicker play. I may use it early!

Day 24

Josh's eye swelled further overnight; and I called Alison Maples DO, our pediatrician. She wanted him seen today; so, I found an English sub for my first class and went to the clinic. Josh's eyesight was great; and it will require ice, head elevation, and time. There is no infection; and no need for antibiotics. Josh was placed on some anti-inflammatory medications (Mobic). While walking out of the clinic to the front door, the pediatrician asked if I wanted to attend a ski party Saturday evening. It is a young millennial group of all types of skiers – from beginners to advanced. They meet for socialization (needed after Covid) at one of the member's houses. The couple hosting Saturday night lived in the Broadmoor area of The Springs. It is potluck and Alison stated she would take care of the food. She would call with the time and details. I mentioned that I had the homecoming game tonight; and a birthday party for Josh to attend tomorrow (I need to get a gift). I honestly could not say no to Alison because she was so nice and beautiful. I know I am not ready for this; but here goes.

The game went as expected. Colorado Sports Academy High School won the game with a well-timed jet sweep that had a monster hole for the flanker to take it to the house. He is our most speedy player with a very low 40-yard dash time. The hand-off and timing were perfect because it froze the linebackers. The linebackers stood their ground and thought it was a fake; they thought the play was in the opposite direction. I noticed both Missy Bradford (reporter) and Alison Maples DO pediatrician were at the game. Neither talked to me because they knew I had a close game requiring my best coaching mind. We had a couple injuries after the game I needed to treat. We decided for both players to attend a Saturday morning orthopedic clinic. I waved at both. One of the coaches noticed I was waving at cute girls and wanted to know what was happening. I said just friends. He gave me whimsical look.

Smitty and I got the kids together Saturday morning for a neighborhood birthday party. I wrapped a squirt gun in a box for Josh to take to his buddy's birthday party down the street. The kids play well together and are of varying ages. This is a great neighborhood because it is laid back, parents are understanding about frisbees and bikes going through lawns, and basically everyone is friendly. Janae would have loved to live in this neighborhood. Sherry and Herb Tompkins arrived for the babysitting – knowing that we had both kid activities and myself a ski party in the Broadmoor at 7 PM. Sherry dug for more information; so, I told her the works. She liked that I was socializing and had a date. I do not know if this is really a date; but it is close. I am getting stronger emotionally – I think.

I honestly do not know what to do regarding the present situation. I talked to my life coach, Nurse Practitioner Sandy Swift, early today. She is available 24/7. Sandy is guiding me into areas of thinking I never imagined. Many guy thoughts are quite simple regarding relationships. I had a couple flings in college and a couple interested young teachers in college; but those relationships never materialized. I have developed two that either one could be a long-term partner. Sandy advised to take it slow, be honest with the other partners regarding your careful development of another relationship, the reality of having three young children, in-laws 50 miles from home, and head coaching/English teaching requirements and obligations. In time it is normal to have a close relationship and possibly marriage. These gals will probably want to have more children and we will be a "blended" family! Personally, I never dreamed of such a phenomenon could be happening to me. I have a ton on my plate with two women wanting to move the relationship along. I am extremely concerned that I will upset one of the other gals; but then again, I am not certain of my desires to enter a long-term relationship and potential marriage.

My situation is tough! As Smitty my neighbor states; it is better to have two gals chasing than zero! I understand that most guys would ideally want just one of these girls chasing them; and that I am apparently a good-looking guy (how that happens I will never discern). Real guys cannot calculate what appeals to a girl regarding looks and what interests a woman. I am just a simple successful football coach and teacher with a love for the English language, literature, and formal writing skills. I will take my time with these relationships. I have experienced two dates and both were female generated. In fact, Janae (my deceased wife) chased onto the Chicago practice field when I did not even know who she was. I am slow in the dating process apparently.

The week appears bright regarding our football team. We are healthy, playing well, and ranked in the top 3 within the state of Colorado 5A Division. Thankfully, there is not a ton of pressure on our team. Many sports columnists (except Missy Bradford) do not take our team seriously. The team we are playing this week has not won, is hungry, and has a strong legacy of winning. I feel our team and coaches are taking this team lightly; and I am worried. I need to ramp our practices, play lots of backups, and ensure that we are clean with our offensive and defensive schemes. The 5-2 defense has confused many teams. We have switched into a 3-4; and on occasion a 3-5 defense with zone coverage. Our defensive coaches and players have responded well to the switching of the defensive schemes and pass/run coverage. I love the balance and mind games we are playing against the opposition. One series of downs or a play can determine the outcome of a game. I have stressed that repeatedly. I am still highly concerned about the lackadaisical attitude of the entire Colorado Sports Academy High School regarding this weekend's away game Friday evening.

The kids are doing well in school. Josh is scoring well on first grade exams and finishing his homework with me nightly quite well. Jake is learning numbers and letters at preschool, and Jaiden is behaving/sleeping/eating well. I am not worried about any of them. They understand that Mom is not returning. I tell them what I can about my life as a teacher and coach. All my kids know that I stress education over sports; and that sports are a manner to improve one's discipline and have a healthy mind and body. I am adapting to being a single dad; and this life is becoming more fruitful. My phone rings and it is Alison Maples DO Pediatrician. I will be nice, thankful, and under-react. Gosh, she is cute and very nice (at least to me). Good night!

Day 26

Tonight, I was worried after that late night talk with Dr. Alison Maples that I would be forced into a relationship. She was cool; and just probing my feelings. Alison is savvy with her words, actions, and ability to be cool under pressure. I am certain she has learned from endless difficult medical situations that being non-committal and having a relaxed attitude is a manner of dealing with interpersonal relationships. Interestingly, as she informed me, that she was nearly walking down the aisle when her relationship abruptly ended surprisingly. I did not go into specifics because it could have been an endless number of issues that her partner had not disclosed. Thus, Dr. Maples is being reserved regarding where our mini-relationship is going and how it advances. That is wonderful for me – no pressure.

The day at school was highly interesting. Many students were struggling with Shakespeare readings and his manner of writing. Shakespeare expanded the English language through structure, new words, intelligent descriptions, and word/phrase meanings. The master had a peculiar method of making the English language work for him descriptively. One of our students with an English accent from Liverpool had a method of talking through a Shakespeare play as it should

31

be spoken. I loved it; but could easily relate how much of the class struggled with Shakespeare. My education consisted of myself knowing in college that William Shakespeare lived from 1564 – 1616. He was a poet, dramatist, writer, and playwright. Shakespeare dominated the English language and created beautiful linguistics. Everyone on the globe should know English and thank Shakespeare. Translations to other languages of his 39 plays, 154 sonnets, and three long narrative poems have occurred historically. Historically, and for better all-around English, I want our students to know and understand basic Shakespeare. Shakespeare is tough; but well worth studying. Life itself is tough as I am discovering! I will enjoy life's fruits and deal with the pitfalls.

I was jogging early this morning before getting the kids arrangements completed. I ran into Smitty down the block and we talked openly again. Smitty is struggling with relationships also; one of the gals in his IT office wants a relationship. He is uncertain to go down that path; because he is her superior. The rules are not vague modernly about office romances. He stated his office is low-key, she is a wonderful gal, and did not feel the relationship would be an issue with the company nor anyone else. People wear blue jeans to work, work from home, and freely discuss life situations and deal with family matters at work. All the boundaries are crossed; but nobody seems to mind. I felt the issues is if she still is working and the relationship travels for a lengthy period. Abruptly, someone ends the relationship; and the former couple must work together. Smitty has thought about all this; but life is a collection of "what ifs." Smitty likes this gal; and they will probably end up together. It appears we all need someone.

I had our coaches meeting and it seemed less intense because of the team we are playing tomorrow night. It was like a week off; thus, I am even more scared of the outcome. It is difficult to prepare your team for a losing squad opponent; but when I discussed our transfer offensive schemes from wishbone to pro-set, all the coaches appeared that there were no problems. I am concerned that this will leak into our team; and we will get our butts kicked. I am probably worrying excessively. A loss is never a good loss I feel. I want to win every game; and somehow, I can will this team into victory. Goodnight!

Day 27

My first instincts at the game Friday night during halftime was to be a "Lombardi" and start screaming at our players. We were down 21-10 at halftime. The opposition's Homecoming was already becoming a celebration beyond a Super Bowl comparatively. Their alumni and fans were screaming loudly. I knew we were the better team; yet, I could not get out of our team and coaches all week to take this opposition seriously. We had defeated some of the better teams in Denver, practiced rigorously all year until this past week, and I could not garner enough emotion to "super-charge" this team. Therefore, on walking to the halftime locker room, I developed an entirely different tactic to fire this team up and get them over the top. We were in Colorado Springs at a high school about 5 miles from Colorado Sports Academy High School. We bused to the opposition's field and had 2 full buses of coaches, trainers, athletic department staff and players. I walked into the locker room and everyone expected myself to begin screaming and have an active pep talk.

I mentioned to drink Gatorade and water religiously, grab a snack, rest for a few minutes, and I would see them on the practice field in 5 minutes. We were beginning preseason practice in a few minutes because we had not practiced meaningfully all week. Everyone knew that. I explained I could handle a loss; but I could not handle poor efforts at blocking, tackling, ball security, kicking, and quarterback play. I informed the team that we were not far from our school; and I would instruct the buses to leave and park near our school empty. If our team cannot block and tackle correctly and with little effort, our team will have plenty of energy to walk home or back to school. The coaches and myself would also walk behind them because we had not prepared them for this lackluster low-level performance. The room was quiet; and I noticed Missy Bradford (Denver news-paper sports columnist) taking notes and recording. I did not care at this point. I left the locker room and said I would have a bag of footballs ready for offensive and defensive drills. I reported that we would be active blocking, tackling, route, and tip drills – just like summer preseason camp. We would practice until the refs told us to line-up for the second half kick.

The nanny called me as I was walking out onto the empty field and informed me that Jaeden (our 2-year-old guy) had a fever and was pulling his ear. I said to use Tylenol and start the antibiotic left over from the last ear infection. I also said to schedule through the internet a drop-in appointment early AM at Alison Maples DO Pediatric practice Saturday morning. If the situation became worse, then inform me by phone. The halftime drills were spirited, vigorous, and the crowd loved the drills as the opposition returned in amazement at what Colorado Sports Academy High School was performing at halftime. Since bands were playing on the field, we used the nearby practice field in the dark and end zones for practice. I wanted a 110% effort the second half, brisk offense, and confusing effective defensive schemes.

We began the second half with a 5-2 defense with corner and safety run and pass blitzes. Our coverage was excellent and we obtained some sacks, turnovers, and negative plays. On offense, our quarterbacks (I played two) were exceptional running and passing (two-way threats). We committed zero turnovers, ran, and passed the ball with balance, and used occasional trickery and deception. Our misdirects confused their linebackers repeatedly. We scored and were ahead (25-21); whereupon, on the last drive we needed a safety blitz and opposite side line-backing blitz to sack their QB for a timely loss. The opposition needed a TD; and we had to stall that drive on our 30-yard line. I arrived home after thanking the team, coaches, trainers and AD staff for their support and efforts. Our mission is to build men through education and sports. We are doing that as I witnessed a great outing by our team. Missy Bradford met me after the game at the high school and wanted some words for the newspaper. I fed her my full stomach of emotions. She wanted a tiny date with a beer. I smiled at her and said perhaps later this weekend. I have a sick child, a nanny that needs to get home, and an early physician appointment for a repeated ear infection. I do believe Missy is wanting to get serious. I need to talk to my life coach, Nurse Practitioner Sandy Swift soon. I will somehow survive.

Day 28

Yesterday was an amazing day. As a football guy, I could not be happier. We are not the NFL; but in real life terms, the game meant something to all our players, trainers, parents, and athletic staff. Our rating climbed to #2 this week as two teams ahead of us lost close games Friday evening. Honestly, I did not feel our team would do this well. We are obtaining maximum effort from our players both on and off the field with few distractions. Missy Bradford's article was on the front page of the Denver newspaper; and throughout Colorado and allied web sites. It was an interesting perspective she wrote at length about the quiet halftime locker room and Coach Wilford Tremby's speech (that is me) during the intermission. The halftime preseason type practice was discussed; and how it spirited our team into a second half comeback. The effort was a 180-degree turnaround. Missy Bradford explained that the plays on offense were stuffed with misdirects and unpredictability. When we should pass, we ran. When we should run, we passed. The defense 100% confused our opposition team throughout the second half as we held them scoreless. The double blitz at the end of the game as the opposing team was driving was a rare call; but had to be completed. We needed to finish the game on defense because I felt they were close to scoring a winning touchdown.

Alison Maples DO Pediatrician examined Jaeden the next morning and concluded that he had a substantial repeated ear infection. If he did not improve, he would be required to have a tonsillectomy, adenoidectomy, and possibly ear tubes. We would continue the antibiotics until this episode resolved; and then reunite with an appointment in two weeks. I left the office as she stared – thinking I would ask her for a rendezvous of some sort – a real date. My God, Alison is cute. I did say we would be "in-touch;" however, that is not stepping up as a serious interaction and follow-up date. I need to level with these gals; and inform both that I need time and am extremely busy to tackle a gal relationship. I still think about Janae; and how I wish she was here. I realize that life is not fair; and to make the most of our existence on earth. I am restarting Catholicism this week and will get the kids into St. Francis Church in Rockrimmon – recommended by fellow Catholic teacher colleagues.

I was jogging after the early pediatric appointment and Saturday coaches meeting. I ran into Smitty. We discussed having a beer tonight while watching some college football at one of our houses with kids and pizza. I agreed. I informed him of my dilemma and he his office romance now beginning. We both are treading in troubled waters with second half romances. The trouble is that I have two; and Smitty has an office parlay which could mean big trouble down the twisted road. The pizza was fantastic as was the comradery. We both committed to openly discuss our life situations. My life coach meeting with Nurse Practitioner Swift today was also excellent; as she mentioned to just take your time. I have not committed to any relationship, girl, or anything else. I am in the non-rushed mode; and things will happen over time that will clarify my future relationships with the opposite sex. The life coach mentioned I really do not know either of these gals intimately or via reputation. Many aspects of their lives remain undisclosed until a serious relationship develops. Thus, I am taking my time, enjoying my Colorado lifestyle, and adjusting to life as a true widower – not bad!

Day 29

I firmly believe that I am in control of my life and cannot let other variables dissuade me from my mission. I am a football coach, English literature instructor, and father of three beautiful boys. I have been dealt some unfairness; yet everyone on this planet must deal with unpleasant stuff. My former wife, Janae, lived a great life, gave birth to three beautiful boys, and made myself a better person. I should be happy, proud, and feel highly fortunate that I by serendipity met Janae. If she had not dropped her purse which caught the turn style at Soldier Field in Chicago, I would not be here in Colorado. I miss my family in Chicago; and of course, they and the school want me to move back. My former state winning 5A football team is barely 500 this year. In deference to the coaches and team, we lost a ton of starting varsity through transfers and graduation. Honestly, if I was coaching the Chicago team today, I do not feel I could do much better. The coaches I left to run the team were excellent. The team, school, and family are all moving on and dealing with me not being present. That bothered me considerably because Janae before she died wanted to ensure her boys were raised in Colorado. I respect her opinion and will 100% live up to her single request. As for myself; she knew I would move on, remarry, perhaps have more children, and become a blended family. I had not given that much thought; but I will adhere to her wishes. We have an early upcoming ski trip with some of Josh's friends. Janae and I had skied a couple times previously in Wisconsin near Lake Geneva and Northern Michigan. We enjoyed the sport immensely; and I was anticipating skiing with her forever down the Colorado slopes. I am dealing.

Matt and Austin, my assistant coaches, came over and we discussed the next week foe. The Denver opponent team is a little over 500, lost some close games, and has a D1 quarterback in their backfield. We are utilizing a 4-6 defense with a monster chasing the quarterback. Our linebackers will cover their tight ends, our safeties are free to roam in zone, and the corners will play man to man with their speed receivers. We will blitz with our monster defender – who will follow the QB to the bathroom if needed. I am worried that Colorado Sports Academy High School is playing above its athletic talent and ability; but our guys have risen to the challenge. We will make the end of the year playoffs; and that is a very positive ending to our first season. I tucked the kids in and told stories after the coaches' film meeting with snacks in our family room. The kids all were playing some kitchen video games I do not understand. Jayden at 2 years of age just mired in the world of fast-moving video games. My assistant coaches are well trained and will obviously be head high school coaches soon. We had a great time; but I can easily discern there's consternation about our team this week. Colorado Sports Academy High School is undefeated; and we feel a thundering and

35

galloping herd of teams chasing us. I told our coaches and team this week: "play smart, play hard, and enjoy the ride."

Day 30

Jacob had a cold today; so, with the fever and ear pulling we were in Alison Maples DO Pediatrics office after school but before practice. I feel she is an excellent physician, obviously wants a guy (potentially me), and wants to do something with me. Our game is Friday night in Denver; and she states after the script for ear antibiotics that she and her medical assistant are coming to the game. That statement threw me for an unexpected loop. I thanked her for coming; and it is inevitable Alison will run into Missy Bradford, my other "kind of" girlfriend. I will call the life coach today; and ask her how to deal with the situation. I am certain the Nurse Practitioner will say to go what feels best; and do not worry about such stuff. Deal with the situation as it happens. It always seems like it is a maddening rush to remate, remarry, and create more family. I do "get" all this; but these gals are intense about their needs. The life coach, Sandy Swift – Family Nurse Practitioner, was quite adamant about me grumbling and grieving about my former wife, Janae. At some point, it is normal to have a girlfriend relationship, probably incur some romance, and potentially wed. The life coach mentioned that Janae also recommended and saw that happening while she was dying. I cannot escape the grief; but with grief, we deal and it fades with time. I am learning life lessons. We remember the good times, our kids, and are thankful for what we had together regarding time and family with my former wife, Janae.

School was exciting because I instructed and the gave a phonics and English test over basics – stuff like adverbs and adjectives and their differences. I informed the class that either they obtained 100%; or they would stay after school for corrections – even until midnight. I received zero parent complaints because that is why students are "stepping up" and attending our school to learn. English is so critical to Western Civilization thought patterns in all disciplines including the arts, math, science, IT, history, communications, and business economics. Relaying your thoughts through verbal exchange and writing is so unique to modern life. Failure to learn and adapt to communication properly is a failed education. I will not allow that to happen to our students. I want all our Colorado Sports Academy high School students to ensure that they are comfortable in relating to English and literature in a professional manner within their family, work, and IT. Without English, nobody advances in the world. A student asked me what difference will this make in his future music career of performing, learning music theory, and teaching the arts. I gave him a simple example of Paul McCartney of the Beatles (>100 pop tunes written and performed). McCartney was truly one of the greatest pop rock composers of all times – everyone knows him because they listen to him perform. Paul McCartney states that his lyrics around which he built musical chords (multiple paired harmonious notes) came about through simple English. Paul McCartney used paired couplets or rhymes with simple English – taught in elementary and high school. It all began with English; it is that basic and simple. We need English to succeed in life!

Day 31

Our Colorado Sports Academy High School Football Team crushed the Denver squad last night. We still had strength and conditioning training for the athletes, training sessions with hot tubs, and a film review with the coaches the following Saturday morning. We played two quarterbacks; and I called plays (non-audible) with QB subs freely. We checked off simply on scrimmage with a QB audible if it was obvious the play was stuffed. Specifically, if our halfback was catching the ball in space or the flats to the right, and the defense was heavy with linebackers and safety covering that portion of the field, our QB called a run to the left. It worked perfectly consistently. I made a couple mistakes and did not expect the varying defensive formations the Denver club effectively utilized defensively. Our team and QBs upon walking up to the line of scrimmage knew the play would be called-off if the defense was right where we were attacking. At times, we witnessed a 3-7-1 defense which is tough to block. Historically, I told our team that 5A football teams are so close in talent that one play may decide the game; and I felt in the second quarter our audible and run right was superb – especially the fullback's block on the linebacker from an audible. The play went for 45 yards when it was 3rd and 4 yards to go. We discussed the use of the West Coast offense – developed by Paul Brown and Bill Walsh of the Cleveland Browns in the early 1970s – leading to the spread offense. The no-huddle offense was perfected by Jim Kelly of Buffalo in the 1990s – disallowing a team to catch their breath, substitute, or properly line-up before the snap. Confusing the defense with both huddles and no-huddle worked well.

After the game I was dealing with parents, injuries, and fist pumps. Alison Maples DO did walk by the bench and said nice game/Coach. She smiled, said I had my hands full, and headed back to Colorado Springs with her friend. I thanked her for coming. My God, she is cute – wearing a beautiful dress – at a high school football game. The coaches all detected some type of relationship, and they smiled as Dr. Maples walked away. One comment towards me (Coach Tremby) was that she is a good catch. I did not care because we won the game handily (40-19). Now I suspect players, coaches, and everyone else will think Dr. Maples and I are a "thing." I will just deal; and at present do not care because we won the game.

Missy Bradford from the Denver newspaper said to me as we were nearing the bus that we would possibly be ranked #1. She mentioned that all the talk around Colorado was about our team and Coach Wilford Tremby. I mentioned that I was happy we won; and that trumps chatter. The coaches mentioned we have come far as a team. Missy suddenly sneered at me with a questioning look. As we parted, she mentioned that this is how you want it…or some sort of degrading comment regarding us. That really caught me off guard; but I understand her feelings and myself not stepping-up. I jumped on the bus and the driver asked if something is wrong? I replied that the reporter is interested in me; but I am not ready yet. The bus driver said there are bumps in all relationships. The reporter is just letting you know how she feels, cares, and is not going down without an expression. I thought that Janae and I really did not have a bumpy relationship; but again, I am now a widower. And maybe Janae and I would have had issues down the road. The playing field now is quite different. Some days I sit and think when the kids are in bed as to how I ended up in North Colorado Springs. I need to get home, tell bedtime stories, have a beer, and think.

Day 32

I rushed home after practice today with Josh taking a swipe across his face while just learning Lacrosse at school in a Saturday morning session. He received a cut; and the school nurse at practice said he would need sutures in the Emergency Room. I will call Dr. Maples DO. She informed me to bring him in with her Saturday morning clinic; as she had immense surgical and suturing experience in her training. We placed Josh in a papoose; and then used some Marcaine to numb the face. An hour later, all the cuts were sewn shut with no dressing and just antibiotic cream. Josh felt great and received a sucker. Alison invited me to another ski party Sunday evening; and I accepted. There is no way I was turning her down with her work on my son and her overall niceness – let along startling beauty. The details she would email me later that day. Perhaps I do need to step up; but I am not certain I am ready for a serious relationship. All adult relationships are serious – they are not: "Let's be friends." I felt good that Josh was healing and he is now a touch gimpy regarding more Lacrosse. I said we would regroup in a couple weeks; and Josh said he would think about it.

My early morning run was met by Smitty walking his puppy. We briefly said hi and he invited me over for a beer to watch football that night. I replied that I did not have the time and was going to a ski party with Alison Maples DO. Smitty thought it was serious; and I did not realize that she is thinking family while I am thinking football. Smitty said take it slow because you need to know stuff about her that is not on Facebook. Smitty smiled and then had a depressed look – stating that he was dumped by the in-office romance. He liked her; and the break-up was quick and unexpected. She is still working there and it is uncomfortable. I felt bad for him; but in the grand scheme I was happy because their relationship could have been a façade. We discussed Monday Night Football at my house after the kids were in bed; and he agreed to bring in some special brew from downtown Denver. We enjoy each other's company. Our kids play endlessly with each other. The neighborhood could not have been better for our kids. Janae would have loved our neighborhood, the sports, skiing, and loved watching our football teams win games. I am still grieving; but I will grieve for life undoubtedly. Off to bed with "The Cat in the Hat."

Day 33

The ski date with Dr. Maples went well. She is certainly serious about a continuing relationship. We had a great time; and most of the socialization mentioned our Colorado Sports Academy High School Football Team. Many of the ski club had been to some of the games; and ski club members were following the team on social media. They seemed to know considerable about my life, previous football team in Chicago, and my former deceased wife, Janae. It seems that the crowd sensed that Alison Maples DO and I are a "thing." Honestly, I am more about winning football games and caring for my three kids than having a true relationship. My life coach, Sandy Swift, LPN, has hung in there with me and wants me to just go with the flow and my feelings. The gist of the counseling has been that life is unpredictable; and opportunities present themselves unexpectedly. Neither Missy Bradford or Alison Maples may not be around if I blow both away from myself. I am months from Janae's death; and it usually requires a year or longer for recovery and reestablishment of a relationship with the opposite sex. I am now beyond 6 months and heading towards a year. I like both these girls equally; and I need to be honest with one or both. Besides, my English/literature class, football team, and kids are plenty on my plate. Janae's parent's, Sherry and Herb Tompkins, are never without intimations regarding Denver's Greenfield Village debutantes. I will admit that Alison was cool regarding my situation; and understandably giving me some room. We smooched at the end of the night; but there was nothing more.

My English class has been all consuming. Understandably, I received a couple administrative parental and student complaints regarding teaching basic English. There were concerns of why we needed to learn the basic four types of adjectives (possessive, interrogative, demonstrative, and compound). There are subtypes; but I wanted our class to be able to know, write, and relate in superb English the basic forms of adjectives. Simply, an adjective modifies a noun or pronoun. The second half of the year we will focus on great readings, writings, and essentially conduct a college course in English literature. I want our students to want to be in our class, reading 2 hours per evening, and writing great prose. This is more important than football. I spoke to the students and parents; and I thoroughly explained that my class may appear overboard – but they will realize in a business/medical/family writing years later that our class allowed them to be precise and articulate with words. Both students stayed; and are reading and writing well. I am trying to obtain college credit for the work in our class. The school administration is working on this aspect of our high school curriculum. There are some hurdles that must be overcome; but, perhaps by the end of the year my students will have a 4-credit college English course attached to their resume.

Josh has a birthday party after school this week, Jake has a pre-school field trip, and Jaiden has a doctor appointment. I will be busy; but it is doable. Time for "Goodnight Moon."

Day 34

The week is flying by with preparation for a supposedly weak Denver football team. We are favored by 21 points; but I feel the game will be close. Our players are tired, overworked at school, and it has been a long season. We are now ranked #1; and everyone is attacking Colorado Sports Academy High School with ferociousness. I fear the worst if we fall behind. I have implemented a jet sweep with both quarterbacks on the field – a play we will call 4-6 times in the game. Our defense will be blitzing on unpredictable downs, and I will play my entire bench since I perceive team fatigue. We have talked about the subject after practice; and most of the team is worried about blowing the season. I have emphasized the season has already been a success, Colorado Sports Academy High School will be in the playoffs, and the coaches and fans could not ask for anything more. Where we end up against tough Denver teams in the playoffs will be determined by our conditioning, focus, and athletic ability on the field. Turnovers will be a key; and I will be emphasizing ball control all week and into the playoffs. Catching a pass modernly is not just handling the ball; it is a squeeze and secure possession into the body with both hands. We should not worry about "going to the house" or a TD. The main fundamental is ball security – especially in a crowded environment with ball strippers. Our running game, handoffs, and pitches must be precise and in-rhythm. Failure to concentrate on the immediacy will lead to turnovers – which decide games.

My doctor's appointment with Jaiden was somewhat disturbing. She heard a heart murmur that had not been present prior. Dr. Maples felt that the murmur was innocent; but an echocardiogram or ultrasound of the heart was ordered at Children's Hospital. Jaiden is not symptomatic regarding the heart murmur; but Dr. Maples is being precautious. Walking out of the clinic door I received all the staff staring at myself – as if I am ready to propose. Obviously, the staff knew there was a ski date and perhaps more. I was dumbfounded by the attention; but far more concerned regarding Jaiden's heart murmur. Upon arrival at home, I ran into Smitty jogging by our house and waved. He jogged over to me and asked if I had read any local social media posts. I replied negatively; and he pulled out his Iphone and revealed to me pictures from the ski party. This picture and the content below imply that Dr. Maples and I are now a real "thing" or couple. I felt that this was impossible to avoid.

I am not a celebrity in my mind. I went into the house and received a call from Sherry Tompkins (Janae's parents). Sherry saw the social media posts which are now in Denver's milieu. Sherry said she was happy that I was dating; but I needed to check-out Dr. Maples previous history. Sherry Tompkins would not elaborate; but I have never been one to invade someone's privacy. And much of what is social media stated is false. I will accept Alison Maples for what she is and presents to myself. Then again, I need to know stuff; and do not want to get involved with someone who may be dangerous. Perhaps, I will just ask Dr. Maples to level with me. I would like to trash this social media stuff; but it will only get worse with time. I need to deal effectively with social media (good or bad). Off to bed because the kids are asleep. Goodnight Moon is lying next to them – they love that book.

Day 35

I am relaxing tonight after the kids are down. Colorado Sports Academy High School has remained undefeated; and has one last opponent before entering the playoffs as the #1 seed. There is a conventional and social media buzz about the area concerning the team. I have tried to keep our team in a controlled relaxed but ready state. Our first game will be the lowest seed to make the playoffs; and then we will begin to hit the more difficult Denver teams which are more athletic, stronger, and faster than our team. The only possible method to win these playoff games against big city teams is to outcoach the opposition. I am certain they have reviewed our plays, gimmicks, deceptions, and audibles on offense and defense. Analyzing all games; with >90% confidence the turnover battle wins the game – all other statistics being equal. I have thought about going back to summer basics regarding ball security and throwing the ball into the stands when there is no clear pass route that is open. Our quarterbacks can be lured into throwing across zones with quick safeties and linebackers. One mistake on a slant route can be met with a pick – 6 and game over. Yet again, I do not want our QBs and team to be timid. There is a balance. I do not mind winning ugly; and that is what we will probably need to accomplish with any playoff game. I am treating this weekend's final game as it if is a playoff game.

Josh has a birthday party Saturday afternoon which I will attend; and the back-up nanny will be here most of the afternoon. Our kids will then attend with me a neighborhood block party – possibly inside depending on the weather. We will have our usual coach's meeting Saturday morning while our elective sessions for the players with the players is conducted. We will have massage therapists, hot tubs, and stretching exercises for all of them. Many kids have chores, jobs, and homework that needs attention. I have instructed them that family, religion, and school have priority; and then the football team. We have experienced nearly 100% attendance at our Saturday morning decompression sessions. I am looking forward to the off-football season. The social media is buzzing about this team. Reporters and others have reviewed my Chicago connections; and thankfully, there is nothing negative being said…until I lose a game or worse yet- get blown out! I want our team to succeed in all ways; as the season has already been a success.

Missy Bradford called late and wanted to run an article about our team and me. I said I would with the caveat that most of the article would be about the football team. I wanted her to discuss the academics and social platforms at Colorado Sports Academy High School. She was very congenial and I could discern that she wanted a get-together of some sort – I guess you could call that a date. She would interview me on Sunday early afternoon after mass at St. Francis. She then asked if she could attend mass with our family. I did not know what to say; but then I said certainly you may. She was so wonderful over the phone that I invited her to the neighborhood block party with families. I know broken- hearted Smitty would be there. I do not know if I did the right thing; but I will find out. I am exhausted – off to sleep.

Day 36

The football game last evening was terrific for the fans. Our win secured our top playoff spot. There was rain and mist. Our team stayed on the ground relentlessly. We were able to score and make our winning extra point kick through the horrific weather. Previously, on the Denver squad, one of our assistant coach's noted a weakness in warmup drills in the middle of their line during kicks. There was a gap between the guard and center. Thus, we instructed our special teams to forge a wedge (even brief) between the left guard and center (weak side of the ball). Our linebacker from the outside would shoot the gap and attempt a block. It worked beautifully; and our team won on that very play early in the 4th quarter (17-16). We managed to grind out a few first downs after a jet sweep touchdown to our weak side with great blocking to secure the game. We had scored the go-ahead TD shortly after their score in the mid-4th quarter. I was impressed with our stamina and fortitude though it was an unranked team. I felt the opposition was quite good and underrated playing high school football at a 500 pace. The ride home from Denver was delightful. Colorado Sports Academy High School Football is my mission; and I am beginning to love Colorado.

Sherry and Herb Tompkins invited me to another Sunday afternoon social at their house next Sunday where I will undoubtedly meet some eligible debutantes from Greenwood Village in Denver. I have understood that this will never end until I am remarried; as Sherry and Herb feel I need to have a wife and mom for the kids. I get all this; but it is tiring and difficult to say no to them. This will be the day after our first playoff game on a Saturday afternoon in November. I will comply, behave, and be a good son-in-law. The Tompkins already are aware of my interactions with Missy Bradford and Dr. Maples. I will need a weekend Nanny for that escapade unless I bring the kids – but as I understand the social to be…it is all adults. I would rather Janae's family be involved than not involved.

Now I am thinking about my English/literature class. My lesson plan for my English class this month is a summation of the readings of many early philosophers. In ancient times, as we do now, there were many arguments about the earth, God, rational thought, human traits, and our existence. I want our students to think about many of these concepts and understand these thoughts began in writings from ancient Greece and Rome. These thoughts and mind patterns are questioning many aspects of society modernly with tangential issues of family structure, wars, education, and religion. The students want to learn; and studying some of the masters who have written well is a form of knowledge they would perhaps never obtain in college.

Occasionally, I receive a complaint regarding cursive; but I inform students and parents that our class is optional and apparently not for everyone. Students will learn English, literature, phonics, writing, and speech – all necessary Western Civilization traits that affect social interaction, work, and family life. The kids need a tuck-in; and are demanding Goodnight Moon again. They are talkative tonight; and like myself are beginning to love Colorado.

Day 37

Our Colorado Sports Academy High School team breezed through the last regular season game and are now preparing for a showdown with a dangerous Denver team. We have them on our home turf; but I do not feel we can relax. This Denver team won a tie-breaker with another team based on an overtime win to enter the Colorado High School Football Playoffs – anything can happen. The game is in a day and a half; and frankly I am a touch nervous. The newspapers have been hounding our players and coaches. I have instructions to be neutral, humble, and respectful. And, being mindful of not giving away insider tips such as our jet sweep, flea flicker, or misdirect plays. Our bootleg QB play to the right or left is effective; but must be called in the correct sequence of plays (when the opposition least expects the play). We have had good communication between the players and bench when we call the play. Generally, I will call it as a RPO (run/pass option) when there is no outside linebacker playing where he should be. Our QBs call off the play or timeout if it is not there (such as a safety or corner blitz or with 8 or 9 in the defensive box). There are some variables because our QBs are track stars; and if we give them a chance to break through the initial wave of defense, they could take it to the house. Considerable success comes from coaching and making the correct play calls and adjustments.

Josh had another ski invite next weekend. This will be tough if we continue to win. The trip is to Keystone Resort; and I am making the trip on Sunday morning. We will try to fit in mass Saturday night after the afternoon playoff football game. Josh is doing well in school; so, our entire family will ascend to the mountains – barring some other factor coming into play. I also have the Sherry and Herb Tompkins party in Greenwood Village the same afternoon. I informed them that we would make it with our kids; as I am dropping the two younger kids (Jake and Jaiden) off on our way skiing. The Tompkins are just glad we are making the party; and it was not a big deal that they are also babysitting while holding a late Sunday afternoon gathering amongst friends. I know there will be eligible debutantes waiting for the right guy to fall into their laps (me). I have spoken to my life coach who has instructed me to go with any relationship that "feels" right. I am not certain what that means; but Sandy, my life coach nurse practitioner, says you will know it when it happens.

I received an urgent call from Smitty down the block. He needs some relationship advice and is bringing up a couple of beers. I am not an expert in relationships; and I have relayed that to him. He does not knock on the door; but just enters (small-town stuff). We sit down and share a couple beers. Smitty is being sued by the female employee with whom he had a crush and it was a brief fling. She is claiming workplace harassment with sexual and emotional abuse with gender discrimination. The fellow co-worker claims that Smitty lured her into a relationship and improperly took advantage of the situation through a romantic relationship. Now she claims PTSTD, drinking heavily to deal with stress, psychiatric visits, and wanting to quit her job with lifelong benefits. Smitty is certain that she has been diagnosed with bi-polar psychosis and depression. Her medical records are frozen; and so is Smitty's case if he cannot find a defense. I could only say it could be worse (marriage). His hired attorney is now requesting the court to release her medical records to determine if this is a pattern or part of her disease. Smitty swears he did not do anything aggressive in or out of work with this employee. I am learning about life through Smitty. Good night.

Day 38

We won the game handily at home with a superb first half – Colorado Sports Academy High School's first playoff win in football. The game was decided on turnovers early. We converted a pick and a fumble into touchdown; and then drove the ball into a successful field goal (leading 17-0) at the half. The opposition fought hard the 2nd half; but we made another TD on a planned bootleg by our quarterback. We won going away (31-12). The newspapers and reporter Missy Bradford treated us well in the Denver newspapers. Alison Maples DO, our kids' pediatrician, was at the game. I said hello to both separately; but both gals know there is something going on besides a relationship with just me – if you can even term our get together as a relationship. They know I am busy; and will probably put the plunge into me when football is finished. The school has asked me to be the assistant basketball coach. I am pondering that pending just getting football completed. My English/Literature course is also very busy; and with kids, it is tough to find the time.

The mass on Saturday night was eventful because I did see Dr. Alison Maples on the other side of the church. I said hello as we walked to the cars; and she praised our team immensely. She mentioned that she was a cheerleader and our cheer team was fabulous with a great crowd. We smiled and left staring at one another. I feel I blew it; but I could not ask her for a rendezvous with my kids present. We must prepare for the ski trip tomorrow morning. I am confused about women as any man will attest. Upon arriving home, Missy Bradford from the Denver sports team as a reporter wanted some more information regarding our next opponent. I informed her that Monday we would be reviewing film and game planning. Missy then began to talk about skiing, Denver parties, and perhaps we need to join forces. I was not ready for any of this; but appreciated her feelings. I just blew another opportunity. I slept on the football game, potential relationships, and the fun ski party at Keystone tomorrow morning. We are leaving at 0530 and the car is packed.

We dropped the younger kids off at 0630 while eating breakfast on the way to skiing (a Colorado thing); and then drove to Keystone. We were the first family on the Gondola; and Josh was so excited. We are making a couple runs and then joining our group for a group ski and then a party at noon atop Dercum Mountain at the Summit House – next to the Gondola. The skiing was fabulous as it snowed most of the day. One of the families had a divorced Mom who tried to kind of "hit" on me. I have enough issues; and I did not like her aggressiveness. Apparently, I must become experienced at dealing with these situations. I still long for my deceased wife, Janae; and highly question our Catholic faith in allowing her to die so early from such a terrible disease. I will probably question our entire existence the rest of my life. Our faith states we do not understand earth happenings well; and I certainly do not. We are on the road to Denver!

Day 39

My day is stuffed with administration and teachers meeting along with preparation for parent – teachers conferences. Colorado Sports Academy High School promotes high achievers in sports and academics. All students must prepare 4 years through sports participation in intramurals, club, or Colorado High School sanctioned sports. The sports go away with declining grades; and students are then on probation. Students attend our high school for both the high level of academics and sports. I have talked to many high school recruits who strongly desire to attend; but have borderline or failing grades. I am not certain that our school is the answer; but strong motivation can overcome some intelligence deficiencies. My English and literature classes focus on the fundamentals; and these fundamental English and literature classes drill the English language into our students' minds. I want the student to walk out of our classes with high grades from love of English and literature; and accomplishing a high level of reading and communication through speaking and writing. Colorado Sports Academy High School is not remedial.

Football practice was brisk as we have a playoff game Saturday afternoon against a Denver foe we barely defeated in a prior contest. Our team is readily prepared and we are nursing a few injuries which should be ready. The parents have been quite accommodating; and I have played the entire squad – with many players "stepping up" when needed. The winning comes from selfless play; and all players and coaches agree that winning involves everyone. I can handle a loss because we have been ranked #1 for 3 weeks. I do believe we can win the state title if we play well. The coaches and myself installed a couple plays no team has witnessed prior on film. We have our two quarterbacks in the backfield for runs and passes. Using the shotgun formation, we can side snap the ball to a running back not directly behind center for a RPO (run-pass option). This play will be practiced heavily and used on 5-7 occasions – hoping to catch the opposition off-guard and confusing the defense immensely.

Smitty came over late for an evening beer after I tucked the kids in with another "Goodnight Moon" read. The kids fall asleep quickly after the last page is turned. I love it; but still wish Janae was here to enjoy the bedtime stories. Someday, perhaps I will understand. Smitty and I shared a couple beers and he caught up to me with some social media Colorado front range chatter. There is some talk of myself and Alison Maples DO having a relationship. It then describes the ski parties and fabricates a few other side issues. Modernly, this is expected. Both Dr. Maples and I will both deal with this in our own manner. Smitty was informing me that I may be required to choose one of the two girls; and the 2 professional gals sharing a relationship with me is taboo. I informed him that there was not a formal relationship due to my reluctance to move forward and grief from Janae's leaving our planet. Smitty was cool and said matters would ultimately fall to my advantage. Our parents never dealt with social media; but in today's world it is something that you can deal with by ignoring. That is my way of handling any positive or negative internet gossip. Smitty and I fist pumped; and as guys promised to watch some football this coming weekend. Smitty has been a close friend and a blessing.

Day 40

We gathered as a family for church on Sunday at St. Francis. Josh entered the Catechism class and I wrestled the other two boys into the pew. Jaiden was crawling under the pew and had a field day meeting fellow parishioners. Church was great but onerous taking young kids. Some of the few acquaintances I have met were encouraging regarding our football team. It is obvious that I am a mini-celebrity because of football. I may be a good coach; but we have been very fortunate with players, parents, and winning close games. As I was climbing into my car after placing seat belts on 3 child car carriers, a fellow student in my English class came running over to my car. We said hello and excitedly she congratulated myself on my engagement to Dr. Maples. I replied that I was not engaged. I asked my student the source of the information. She said it was spread throughout social media this morning. I just stared and said it was untrue and that is just something I will have to confront and deal. The kids were asking what is happening on the way home. I mumbled misinformation and then said somebody said something false about Dad. Josh then asked what he heard about Dr. Maples means she will become our new mom? I said at present we were just friends and nothing more.

The kids immediately upon returning home had a lunch snack and traversed the neighborhood to play despite bad weather. I was prepared for the early snow along the front range with 3 sleds. Our dog Spark was able to pull Jaiden along slowly; but not much more. Thereafter all the kids came to our house for after play snacks and collectively play video games. The nanny arrived as I said bye to the kids and somewhat grudgingly drove to the ski party at the Broadmoor - invited by Dr. Maples. I met here there and she was grinning and openly said do not sweat the social media. She remarked that none of this would be a "thing" if I was not winning football games against Denver teams. Winning football games in Colorado Springs is not that big of a deal; but beating serious Denver squads grabs everyone's attention. The party was wonderful with great food and people; and nobody discussed the internet chatter. I gave Dr. Maples a big smooch before we went our separate ways. I am sure when I discuss our relationship with Smitty, he will be consumed by knowing stuff not on the internet about Dr. Maples. We are where we are now; and the past remains the past. I frankly do not care if she robbed 50 banks. Dr. Maples has class and treats me with respect and love. I may be starting to change. Goodnight!

47

Day 41

School work has been increasingly tough with grading papers, administering tests, teacher workshops, and parent – teacher conferences. Most of the parents want to discuss football; so, I must steer them back to academics. There are few academic problems at Colorado Sports Academy High School. Occasionally, we have a student who is not college prep. At this juncture, I talk to the parents and student together and we collectively decide what is best for them. A few schools in the area have a trade school course curriculum; and that is the route that non-academic students should tackle. It is so frustrating to tackle essential college level courses when there is not motivation or a professional desire for college. Our system within high schools for many years did not appreciate the vast differences and needs of students. The amount of reading, writing, and studying required in our classes is immense. Inability to have the learning desire prompts academic failure; and leads to loss of confidence in later life.

Smitty was over for some football watching after our kids went to bed. We discussed some of the preparation for the upcoming championship game after our last late-minute win to get to the finals. The team we are playing at home is far superior in talent and legacy than Colorado Sports Academy High School. The game has been delayed by a week due to a bomb threat that may have involved some of the Denver team's football players. That will not affect our preparation because we will never know who will line-up until kickoff. Smitty's recommendation after watching our team's talent was to continue to use a double blitzing scheme in various schemes. One of the defensive plays had a linebacker and corner blitzing from the opposite sides. We have that as a standard play; but Smitty (who has coached some football in his younger years), felt that lining up a linebacker on the line and dropping him off at the snap into the outside linebacker position – maintaining at least the required 3 on the defensive line – was an old play that needed to be revitalized. After we finished a couple beers I slept on his coaching recommendations.

Day 42

Missy Bradford from the Denver paper called and wanted to know my feelings about the championship game being cancelled and Denver football players possibly being suspended. I felt that would make little difference because the opposition was so stocked with great players. Many on their 2nd string would start on our team because of their athletic ability, power, and speed. I could ascertain there was some terseness in her voice; as we have not been together for a month. I am certain she knows of Dr. Alison Maples and myself. We all must deal with life's bumps and fluid relationships. Ending, she asked if she could watch practice without any recording. I advised her not to attend because players and coaches know she is from Denver; and would be considered a spy. She countered that she was attending our opposition's practices and had sealed lips. I finally crumbled and allowed her to attend one practice session – thinking this was good to maintain media relationships.

I have received endless amounts of fan encouragement, new play and scheme recommendations, and have my assistant coaches all wanting to mend our subtle deficiencies to avoid defeat. I am working with everyone; but have my own ideas regarding avoiding turnovers and keeping our team in the game with a chance to win. I know we will not overpower this team; and must use expert timely play calling to gain advantages on offense and defense. I am still thinking of Smitty's recommendation of a double blitz with linebacker coverage by subbing a linebacker on the defensive line – having him commit at the snap to the 2nd level of defense to cover the outside flat. That would require our best athlete. The confusion with a defensive lineman leaving for the flat and a blitzing linebacker on the outside is intriguing. I will discuss the scheme with my assistant coaches. As I am falling asleep, Dr. Maples calls and wants to attend another ski party Saturday night. I would be her guest at her home. I responded positively as we small-talked about the game being cancelled and moved to the next weekend. My appointment tomorrow morning with Nurse Practitioner and life coach Sally Swift RN will be positive since I am moving forward with a relationship – with all the risks of life's entanglements, and issues of from having more children to being dumped. I need to move on with my life deal better with the grief over Janae's death, and perhaps get the kids a new mom – "I think."

Day 43

The days leading to the state 5A Football Championship are escalating with excitement and fear amongst the student population, fans, players, cheerleaders, and player parents. I have been hearing things that do not normally occur such as: What happens if we fall behind by 30 points, what if we are blown out, or we are treading in Denver football territory where we do not belong. I am throwing the entire playbook at this Denver squad. They will not have seen some of our wishbone, I formations (with 3 backs), pistol backfield, unbalanced lines or having two QBs in the backfield. If the opposition calls timeout for an adjustment; we win because I will change the play during the timeout. On defense, we are using unbalanced lines, varying blitzes and will have team speed to catch their scrambling QB – forcing the play to the middle of the field. I am strict regarding maintaining coverage on the edges. All linemen will have their hands in the air during pass rushes to blind the opposition QB and force turnovers. If Colorado Sports Academy High School loses, we are going down swinging. Though everyone in Colorado Springs is worried, I faced the very best high school teams in Chicago and outmaneuvered them by planning and executing. Our practices preceding the game's delay are phenomenal.

I talked to my life coach and she mentioned that I am transforming, resolving grief, and headed in the correct direction regarding an opposite sex relationship. The life coach feels comfortable that I am resolving the deep-seated guilt, frustration, and severe grief accompanying a spouse loss. She mentioned that I cannot drag this somber mood and anger into the next relationship. We all have many mind clogs that need to be resolved virtually on a never-ending basis. Football is the very least of my worries – though I do not express that to anyone except Smitty. Preparing for a big game is not a new experience for myself; and I perform well knowing what I am facing. I am confident if our team performs well, we will win the game and have an undefeated season. Our players are 110% committed. Many players are discussing playing college football – they love the sport considerably. Thankfully, our team's school grades have not been an issue with the entire team.

My kids are performing well for school, pre-school, and with the nanny. This has worked well; and our neighborhood has pitched in with periodic help since our kids have become leaders of the subdivision kids' play team. The kids play endlessly after supper until bedtime; and these are real fun child games. It is common to have neighborhood late night snacks with popcorn and ice cream before everyone retires. Everyone is smiling; and Janae would be so happy. They still love Goodnight Moon as their favorite book. Goodnight Moon is now memorized with myself. I still do hear progressively from the kids about getting a new mom. Josh says everyone but Jake, Jaiden, and himself has a mom. I said I am working on it as they fall asleep. Football is life; but our family is real life!

Day 44

After I gave the nanny instructions, I hurriedly went to our football field for the final championship game. The field was stuffed with fans 2 hours pre-game. Our players were assembled and we had a brief chalkboard meeting before warmups. The team and coaches recommended repeatedly having two QBs in the backfield (equal talent with both having RPO (run-pass options). I said we would use this strategic play depending on the score, prior success, game situation, and what my gut told myself. I was not opposed to running an entire drive with 2 QBs on the field. Understand if we have a hot back that is grinding 8 yards a carry, we will beat that to death until the runner is stopped. I love wearing defenses down until they react with 8 or more players in the defensive box.

The game remained close until we forced a turnover strip after a crossing pass reception. Our linebacker ran the fumble back putting us in the lead. We unexpectedly on the ensuing kickoff recovered an on-side kick. The 2 QB backfield set produced a monster run for a score; and we never looked back. Our fundamentals were tremendous; and we walked off the field with a perfect 14-0 record. The locker room was ecstatic with joy, sweat, and media. Missy Bradford gave me a kiss that was more than just a congratulations. Honestly, inside I did all this for Janae. My feelings are that I care a ton more for Janae at this moment because she followed me all through the last winning season in Chicago. These two girls chasing my heart are wonderful; but relationships to me are now just different. I cannot describe my feelings; but inside I feel I need a relationship and the kids need a mom. My life coach continues to inform myself to tackle one day at a time – easier said than done.

After all the hoopla and vigor of winning a state championship, I was the last one to leave the locker room after a party was planned at one of the assistant coach's homes tomorrow evening. One of our cornerbacks had an extremely sore wrist he did not inform us about since the first quarter. He intercepted a tough pass in the flat in the third quarter. His parents were divorced recently and his dad was not in the state. His mom asked me to examine him; and I said we need an Xray tonight. The player's mom had a little one at home and I told her I would take care of the injury and bring him home after the Xray and treatment at Penrose Hospital. My nanny was good with staying late because it may be 0200 or so before we get home. I walked into the parking lot and Dr. Maples was there with a big hug and congratulations. She wanted to tag along to the hospital. This is how Janae and I had our first date – taking an injured player to the ER. Alison Maples DO is certainly supportive. She is going to the post-game party tomorrow night - after we finally with the wait and treatment for a fractured wrist - got our cornerback home at 0300. The non-displaced small distal radius fracture should heal over the next 6 months. What a wonderful day!

Day 45

The next day after the championship game was tumultuous. We had a preschool party for Jake; and then a birthday party with Josh. I had to get gifts for all these celebrations; so, I went on line to calculate what to bring and where to get stuff. I ended up going to a Super Target and successfully purchased age specific Lego toys that morning. I am running with Jaiden having a diaper rash and crying a ton. Where is Janae when I need her? My thoughts race regarding having "new mom" stuff. I am getting that from all sides – including kids, Janae's parents, and my teacher and coaching colleagues. People are just trying to be nice; but I truly am skittish regarding a deep committed relationship. Yes, it would be nice to have a woman of the house; but all this comes with immense commitment, time, courtship, weddings, honeymoons, and another family. Perhaps we are all set where we are as a family; and I should not rush into such love and madness and risk a relationship with an assortment of baggage. Janae and our relationship were nothing but love without restraint – I was fortunate and very lucky – after watching good couple relationships turn sour.

What happens if my fiancé is also ravaged by disease, has a miserable family I need to periodically confront, or is a mental health problem herself that surfaces after marriage? Thereafter, I am then stuck with pills, doctor visits, and endless encounters dealing with controlling psychiatrists and her mind. I think of Smitty – his wife having to be committed to a state hospital – totally uncontrollable – though perhaps no fault of her own. I guess life has its risks and some women will do what they need to do – including concealment – to capture a supporting alpha male. These are my inner thoughts that do not stray and must be written per Janae's directive. I am enjoying writing the diary. It is my consummate mental health treatment – along with my life coach, NP Sandy Swift. These facts of my life keep me going and not treading water.

While I am dealing with the drop-offs and pickups at the kids' parties, Jaiden vomits green tinged fluid. His clothes are a mess; and I need to rush home to change his clothes and clean him. He was so good through all this; and we are strongly bonding. Jaiden even says Mom when I am the dad. While I am driving with my phone on its mount, I am receiving college coach recruiters galore texting, calling, and emailing myself. They are quite cordial, have great offers, and I am fully expecting this barrage – like the coaching offers I received after winning the Illinois football championships. I politely reply no - despite knowing I can name my price. I am not certain I want to enter those upper end coaching channels – because it is never ending. There are name and no-name programs offering considerable perks - from assistant to head coaching positions. I was trained to be a teacher of English, literature, and composition. That is where my interests lie. Coaching is great; and an instructional tool. I do not want desire to chase coaching positions as a never-ending spiraling endeavor. I could establish a web site and promote playbooks; but again, there is banter, blogs, and time with secondary work.

Smitty came over for some Sunday night football. My day was so busy with the coach and team party -moved to late Sunday afternoon. Dr. Maples attended with me; and we had a great time. Jaiden's GI disease quieted with some Pepto-Bismol. I could discern that Dr. Maples wants us to be a serious relationship; but I just do not know. I know I cannot fend off a beautiful woman who wants seriousness in the relationship forever. Smitty tells me I either need to break it off and find another pediatrician or go with it. Smitty and I discussed the successful use of a 2 QB backfield set and how we would blow away college and pro teams with the mass confusion when receiving a side angled snap. The beer from a Springs craft brewery Smitty brought to our house after the kids fell asleep tasted great after an immense suspenseful weekend!

Monday morning, I was met with many high fives and fist pumps from faculty, students, and administrators. The assistant coaches on the football staff rightfully are receiving offers for head coaching positions; and I suspect I will lose 2-3 coaches who want to enter the coaching carousel market (good for them)! My assistant coaches have earned the respect and integrity amongst Colorado and the national coaching fraternity. Colorado Sports Academy High School won the upper division High School Football Championship without recruiting a single player. Our players attended our school for the high level of academics and excellence in sports. Our first year was a success with many other sports excelling well amongst state powerhouse athletic programs. We have a long way to go with practice fields, sports funding, swimming pool, and budgeting with sanity our athletic programs admixed with academics. We now have Denver students wanting to attend our school. We are private; but receive some peripheral state funding – which may cause an upcoming nexus issue with church/state entanglement. There is a strong push to incorporate religion into our school. I will allow the administrators and parents to deal with that issue. I am not against the issue as it may prevent violence, suicides, failing grades, or providing a life scheme for many susceptible students. Religion may counteract endless and mindless negative social media barrage – provide a path for many students.

The composition lesson today was writing in the first person – stating your own thoughts. I want our students to be able to express themselves in the first person because they will be in all employment endeavors. The first person is not unlike my diary – I write what my mind thinks. All students are on-board with the ideas in our classroom and want to learn. Our school strongly desires a pattern of informing students not to attend if they cannot handle or are not motivated to learn academics at Colorado Sports Academy High School. Writing composition is a strong part of our curriculum. We will be continually changing the writing style and I expect some authors from this class. I remember writing a short story when I was in high school that won a scholastic magazine award. This was my start and my love of English, Composition, and Literature studies. Despite the Artificial Intelligence that can produce a book report or term paper in seconds; the mind needs to be trained and become a learned bank of information. Perhaps I could be like a Joe Paterno at Penn State and teach English while coaching – but his ending did not finalize well. I am actively being a real teacher and coach – the entire package at Colorado Sports Academy High School. I am in my element!

Jaiden became very ill and I had an emergency appointment with Dr. Maples. She ordered a CT scan of his abdomen, admitted him to Children's Hospital in Colorado Springs, and called general surgery. The surgeon felt the CT scam would only confirm appendicitis; and my little guy needs an appendectomy. The operation went well, Dr. Alison Maples is now my hero, and I heartfully thanked the hospital staff with some purchased cookies A couple nurses knew of our football team and wanted to discuss having 2 QBs in the backfield. They mentioned that a couple friends had student athletes on our football team. I was more than happy to talk football because they had done such a great compassionate job caring for Jaiden – healed and ready for home. Dr. Maples and I are having a late-night supper after the kids are down. I have a neighbor 14-year-old gal who loves to babysit. Alison Maples made the date so after Jaiden's cure, I am not running away from someone who does their job well. The relationship is starting to turn the corner. Maybe, I will go with it!

Day 47

Football is through and the offers are pouring in through the school, email, faxes, and texts. Incredibly during school hours, a prominent top 10 football program who is never not in the news showed up after school was dismissed. I was grading papers and the athletic director and university president were welcomed into my classroom by the school superintendent. Everyone tended to know who these people were; and there were interested bystanders outside the room – anticipating news that I am leaving for the glory of coaching a legacy college football program. Word spread like wildfire through the Colorado Sports Academy High School family. It was assumed the next day I was gone after the school year ended – if not before. I do have a year-to-year contract with the school district which I am honoring. Obviously, I could be released by the school board for extenuating circumstances; but deep-down I am not one to dishonor commitments. The college AD and university president were very cordial, lucrative, and made an offer 99% of coaches could not refuse. Though I am honoring Janae's pledge for me to raise the children in Colorado, I need to rethink this entire scenario. Apparently, I should be proud over the rooftops with winning a Colorado State High School Football Championship in our first year – stealing it from Denver. The reality is this winning is clouded with the extraordinary grief as an unexpected widower. I informed this college football recruiting team of the AD and college president what I was feeling and dealing. They understood. The head coach of this college had just been released due to a reasonably good; but not great record. I understand; but I am also a teacher of English and Literature at heart.

Beyond the college coaching ranks are the professional ranks. The phone calls came from a few professional teams regarding assistant coaching positions. I listened, the money and perks were fabulous, and this was an entirely different level of commitment year-round coaching, scouting, drafting, attending pro days, and combines in Indiana yearly. I would be gone from home a ton. Many of the coaching jobs came with nannies, traveling perks, and incentives based on player and team productions. The coaching professions knew their business well; and many had reviewed films of our 2 quarterback sets. There were many questions regarding the 2 QB set with men in motion, side snaps, bootlegs, and fakes. I replied were had a few twists depending on the defense; but we willingly made the plays quite simple. Two running/passing QBs with RPO (run-pass option) ability, allows immense flexibility and surprise into our offense – including the 2nd QB being a runner and pass receiver. Both QBs are taking hits relentlessly; and must be as durable as a running back. I am probably more confused now after the visits.

Missy Bradford from the Denver paper called and wanted to know where I was coaching next year. I replied I did not know; but most probably I am staying in Colorado Springs with 3 little kids. Missy jokingly mentioned they need a mom…. but I understood that as a serious gesture. We parted ways amicably – as she already knows about my relationship with Dr. Maples. I could discern she was frustrated. I almost said there are 8 billion people in our world – meaning there are 4 billion males. I am not the only male. I do like Missy Bradford; and she would make a great wife. I get Janae's mom does not like her because she was not from Greenwood Village – Denver money. I have many things to think about; and we will discuss with my neighbor Smitty tonight over a beer when our kids are finally tucked in bed.

Day 48

My text sounded loudly this morning. I prepared breakfast for the kids and prepared them for school. Josh is performing well in all-day kindergarten; Jake is learning rapidly in preschool; and Jaiden is the nanny's pet child. The nanny is ill today so the substitute nanny is on her way. I am so fortunate to have such great schools and nanny services. I do not know if I could ever procure such a great set-up as I now utilize. I have a supportive classroom, student body, administration, neighborhood, and child services. It does not get any better……. well, unless I get the kids a new mom. A new mom would more than likely pressure myself into jobs that pay multiples of my present income. A coaching carousel follows myself throughout the rest of my life; and I am chasing money and prestige. A new wife likely would push me into much higher paying coaching jobs to allow solvency and security. Our kids are young enough that a move would not be hampering. These are all questions that I could have solved with Janae. She is one of the few spouses or persons in my circle that would say "stay put." Janae is not in our world; and again, I need to move on. Perhaps someone in the neighborhood would have disliked our family; and Janae would have said take a job in Houston or San Francisco – could not be worse. Additionally, our neighborhood could dramatically change since Colorado Springs is quite a mobile community – as are most IT communities. My life coach, Sandy Swift NP, says go with the flow and let your gut decide what is best for your family….and your heart decide what is best for your relationship.

Smitty talked a ton last evening regarding his bipolar divorced wife who was committed. Apparently, she has improved and is moving out and wants her kids back (full custody). Smitty feels the kids will die; and he has months of upcoming litigation battles. After we finished dealing with a drained bank account to properly maintain his family and deal with a mentally ill former spouse, it was all football talk. We discussed the offers; and Smitty feels I need to visit a couple of these college or pro camps. He remarks that once a losing season hits Colorado Sports Academy High School, there will be vultures wanting my coaching removed. Despite winning a 5A high school football championship, a coaching job is never safe. There are now some articles and discussion in the football and sports media regarding the 2 QB setup. I have been asked to participate in some skype television and podcasting sessions. Smitty and others feel it is genius what we have done with our backfield in single-wing T, wishbone, and stacked I-formations. As head coach we used this in Chicago which tricked the entire town. In Colorado, the formation fooled the entire state. It is just a matter of time before defenses adopt appropriate defenses. I know how to defense a 2 QB set-up; but I am not saying a word. It required 30 years of college football before the wishbone offense became defensible. It matters how your backfield performs – using their athletic skill, strength, and speed to win the contest.

Dr. Maples and I are having a small dinner in South Denver Saturday evening at a local famous steak house. She has already texted me as to where I may be coaching next year. She states the town is buzzing. I reinforced to her that no decision has been made; and that our family will probably stay in Colorado Springs. That generated a thumbs up on the text.

Day 49

Jaiden came down with a fever and ear pulling today. I need to get him to the pediatrician. I call Dr. Maples and she is not in the clinic today. I asked if she would be there tomorrow or in the evening clinic. The receptionist remarked that Dr. Maples took a leave of absence from the clinic; and her return is questionable. Whoa! I asked what happened and the receptionist said she was not at liberty to discuss privacy information. I totally get that; but am wondering where she is and why she is not responding. Thus, I call her on the phone and there is a recorded message that I will get back to you. Something has happened – either an illness, family, or personal issue. I do not know where this is leading our relationship – because it was beginning to get serious (as she wanted). One would think she would allow me to know what is happening. I do not know her family – and therefore cannot discern where to go. Perhaps something "bad" has happened?

I went to the clinic and received some amoxicillin; and the substitute pediatrician mentioned that Jaiden may need ear tubes and a tonsillectomy and adenoidectomy. We will determine over the next week how Jaiden recovers from these repeated ear infections. The nanny came to save me so I could get to my English class. We have a big test on William Shakespeare today. This will be difficult for the students; but I want my graduates knowing about the world's greatest playwright. Thoughts are racing through my mind regarding Alison Maples DO as I administer the test. I can easily discern the tenseness within the room. As I am handing out tests, I state that our goal is to recognize Shakespeare and his genius with language, syntax, grammar, and communicative abilities. Why did Shakespeare write so many great plays that have withstood centuries?

I encounter the athletic director as I am walking the halls during the test to ease the student test taker's mind. I preached the honor system; and that if an answer was unknown, we would retest until the entire class was perfect. The AD asked why I was not in the classroom; and I replied that I would be causing stress by staring at test-taking students. He understood the honor system. I suspected this was about coaching basketball, tryouts, cuts, and making tearful student athletes and parents. The boy's frosh basketball coach stepped down from the position due to family issues (divorce). Thus, the AD needs an emerging sub; my name was added to the mix. I told myself I would not get into hoops (one of my pure loves). I informed the AD that I never cut student-athletes and would play all 50 on separate squads. The AD felt that was undoable; but I said everyone would play on some squad – be it 1st string to 5th string. We would somehow find gyms, time, parent coaches, and play a ton of hoops. The AD left impressed. I entered the room where my test takers all were in a state of shock, The athletic director left hearing me state that we all are learning Shakespeare – along with many other great writers. They stared as I said: "If you get through me, you will easily pass any college literature of English class!"

Day 50

Smitty was over the next day; and we hashed as guys the Alison Maples situation. Smitty foretold something potentially devastating (illness, custody battles, crime, or family issues). The entire scenario is weird. I may never actually see Alison Mapes DO again. I have heard of couples separating when one of the partners goes "poof." This is what is happening. I am probably truly "dumped!" There were no clues; nor any hints of misgivings, illness, stress, or alarms sounding. Smitty did not feel I should take on the frosh basketball squad – too much toil and pressure from students, administration, and parents. I retorted that I was accustomed to the noise, I love sports, and it is a way to keep my mind off Janae's early departure from our world. The kids (Josh, Jake, and Jaiden) all have adapted to our new life with a nanny and my coaching/teaching jobs. The "new mom" thing will come; it is just a matter of time. I cannot marry to just marry. The gal taking on 3 step kids is a big hurdle – it is almost undoable. Smitty agrees; but acknowledges that if she loves you, that will trump any hurdles.

The AD called and we agreed on a coaching fee, structure, and the ability to "coach" the team using Colorado Sports Academy High School's basketball schemes from the head coach. The head coach may be thrilled or perhaps intimidated having me on the basketball staff. I will not coach girls – far too many issues (guilty until proven innocent). The rumors were swirling; and now 75 kids are vying for the frosh team. I will solve this with a brief parent/student conference – emphasizing there are no cuts, everyone will play a ton of basketball, and they will learn the sport for life. I will need parental help; and most of our games will be intrasquad scrimmages if the opposition cannot play multiple strings. We will play outside or wherever a basketball court exists – potentially half-court driveways.

I am enmeshed in sports; and will need electric – shock therapy to remove me from the love of sports and coaching. I am already thinking about spring football. There are immense happenings surrounding myself; but the kids and our family are doing well. Smitty agrees as we guzzle another beer before retiring. Smitty wants me to play on video repeatedly the double pass QB set with the lateral and subsequent pass play that mirrors a run – and would fool even Vince Lombardi. The phone rings as I am checking on the kids and about to retire. It is from an elite college program that is offering coaching NIL money with all the perks. He remarks that he knows I am sitting still for now; but encourages me to take a weekend trip to view the immaculate situation. There are boosters that would have you settle for nothing but the best for you and your family. I settle in and begin to think. If Janae were here; she might just say – go where your heart belongs coach. I will stew on this offer. Good night!

Day 51

The coaching offers from college and professional ranks are pouring into my life via mail and email. Smitty and I have been talking immensely about money, girls, football, and life. My job in North Colorado Springs, Colorado has been wholesome and satisfying from a coaching perspective. I love the football team and athletics at our startup school (Colorado Sports Academy High School). The students are driven and motivated to succeed in both the classroom and within the sports' fields. Virtually everyone plays a varsity sport or intramurals. I am respected within the school; and my love is English and literature. If I packed a moving van with our kids and moved to say Penn State, I would lose the gratifying accomplishments of teaching youth academic skills good for life. I cannot do everything; yet, money matters. The issue with myself is that I am looking at multiples of my present salary. My football team could be 0-12 next year and beyond. A short leash exists for coaches modernly. I could end up just as a high school instructor with no team to coach. A social virus could infect our upcoming teams; and I could be out of coaching in 1-2 years. Thus, I am considering some of the mega offers to coach college or the professional ranks. A move would be required; and though our kids could handle this at a young age, they are prospering in Colorado.

The basketball practice with 70 frosh boys on the squad was interesting. I elected no cuts for the team, we would play 7 days/week, and the starting lineups would be determined after practice success and motivation. Parents were in astonishment; but I have recruited parents to coach lower-level squads with ongoing scrimmages and play v other 2nd and 3rd string teams along Colorado's front range. A ton of hoops will be played by our freshman; and guys that were on lower-level teams will emerge. I want the team and every individual to truly enjoy basketball – and keep playing well into their adult life. I have a few pet peeves in coaching basketball. Specifically, since modern kids shoot 3s like they eat hamburgers, I 100% want switching to occur on picks on top – near the 3-point arc. Below, I want players to fight off screens over the top. Despite mismatches, players today are far too speedy to not find creases to hit 3-point shots. It is a male power grab to fight over screens; however, considerable energy is wasted and teams ultimately develop windows and creases for jump shots and drives to the hoop from the top arc. Stopping the play with a switch surprises basketball offenses; and reliance on avoiding a foul or trailing player is too steep a standard – just switch.

I have not heard one word from Dr. Alison Maples, supposedly our pediatrician and my girlfriend. It has been a few days; and everyone (including social media) is quiet. This could be an illness, crime, or personal matter. There is zero on the social media platforms – which I rarely consult. Perhaps it is for the better – but it would be nice to know where her life is without a word to myself. I do care for her. I need sleep. Good night!

Day 52

The basketball team is now divided into varying skill levels. I coach the top 15 players; and that can switch amongst the frosh based on their ability, maturation, and drive. I saunter down to the lower strings and maintain contact with emerging players. The parents and players get it – most of these players would be cut and never play basketball again (sad). We are starting games on off nights with multiple teams playing – many intrasquad games on multiple gyms. The explosion of basketball has garnered immense school interest – with many more fans at these frosh scrimmages and matchups than the varsity games. Cheerleading has countered with many matching squads. I love it! The school coaches and administrators have been impressed at the level of play; and our teams in the future could compete at a high level in 5A Colorado basketball. Parents have been highly supportive. I have had a couple single moms make subtle "hits" on myself (I think). I have enough girl issues now. I do not need to tangle the girlfriend and potential subsequent spouse issue with another parent relationship – that is a conflict of interest in coaching to a degree. An unwritten rule is that you do not date high school player's parents. That is coach's creed. I am not going there.

Also, I am not into the prior divorce and kids' baggage coming with a relationship. Life should be simple; and if your loved partner robbed 50 banks, has 6 former husbands, or 15 kids – it should not matter. Love is love; and just deal together with your partner's past and present issues. We all have issues – my issue is that I may never overcome the grief of my deceased wife at a young age from metastatic breast cancer. I should have been more aggressive, and together despite younger ages than screening recommendations, I should have demanded earlier diagnosis and more aggressive treatment. In Janae's case, we waited too long before discovering a malignant mass. The hell with the insurance company guidelines and restrictions on mammography. Janae could have incurred a double mastectomy at a young age and been alive. A simple breast lumpectomy and radiation did not stop her unknown other small tumors. That was an aggressive option; but the correct option. I need to stop blaming myself and overcome grief. My life coach, Sally Swift, nurse practitioner, has been tremendous. At least she has placed me into the dating mode.

Our kids continue to do well. Jaiden has healed his ear infections with tubes, tonsillectomy and adenoidectomy, and antibiotics. Jake has so many pre-school friends that once a month we have a party in our backyard – he loves it and the backyard parties maintain his needed popularity. Perhaps I am over-doing kid stuff because they do not have a mom; and everyone else does have a mom. Josh has been skiing with some other friends and I have participated when I can get to the slopes. He loves skiing, is popular and doing well in school academically, and never stops talking about wanting to have a mom. I just mention it will happen when the right woman enters my life. I just tell the kids as a widower that our family is different; and I am both the mom and dad. I will get through this stage of my life.

Goodnight Moon was again read to the kids prior to falling asleep. Smitty came over for some beer and hoops. He has interest in another office gal; and we again discussed the pros and cons of dating within your job sphere. Smitty says it is very different; but I counter that there are endless issues; but it appears both parties need opposite sex relationships. Smitty brought the article from one of the IT sports departments discussing Wilford Tremby's double quarterback offense. Guys in the professional and college ranks are looking at this new football offense as the new "West Coast Offense" akin to 49ers Coach Bill Walsh. The 2 QB set certainly worked for Colorado Sports Academy High School. Perhaps we have started a football movement of perpetual changing offenses – not the dual threat QB, but the dual threat backfield. These football times are exciting. A couple writers mentioned our double and delayed blitzes. Smitty and I love to talk sports. As I led him to the door after a couple of beers, Dr. Alison Maples called – Oh My God!

Dr. Maples and I had a lengthy discussion last night – overdue regarding her disappearance. She is a responsible doctor and girlfriend. I had no idea if Alison Maples was in trouble, went crazy, or had an illness few were aware. When I talked to her, the voice was strained; and she had just finished a procedure at the Mayo Clinic. According to Alison, she has a rare lymphoma – blood disorder. She is obtaining advanced chemotherapy and will be there for another couple weeks. She is weak, lost her hair, her weight has shrunk, and she is in poor spirits. Dr. Maples went into Medicine and Pediatrics because she had childhood lymphoma; and was not expected to live. The radiation, surgery to protect her ovaries during treatment, and chemotherapy helped immensely. She has done well with periodic cancer checks for years. It is obvious that her caring for our kids relates to her being a patient. I am in a state of shock; but understand why she did not inform me or others excepting her family and clinic associates. I am in a query because I should fly out to Rochester, Minnesota and visit her. I am in the middle of coaching, have three young kids, and she said family and friends were there. Alison did not want me there until she recovered. I will see her upon return.

School the next day was depressing because there were complaints from parents regarding the strings of basketball players (7 teams). All the frosh are playing a ton of basketball in varying gyms and outside in good and bad weather. I explained this to everyone at the beginning of the season; and the JV and varsity coaches are all in with playing kids without sport cuts. Many kids would be wandering in malls and parks instead of playing disciplined basketball. I cannot make everyone happy; and if your child is not playing enough basketball, then I do not know where they would go to obtain more hoops. Frosh are playing ball 7 days/week. Scrimmages and intra-squad games have been well attended and competitive. There are always issues about who starts because on a football team there are 44 starting positions counting special teams. Basketball only allows 5 starters and a few bench players. At the top high school 5A level, the competition is extreme. I doubt Denver schools are playing participation ball – neither is Colorado Sports Academy High School.

Jaiden had a croupy cough today; and I made an appointment at the pediatric clinic with Alison's sub doctor. He was quite competent and appeared (with diplomas on the wall) to be taking over the patients and Alison's practice. I asked when she would return; and the sub doctor mentioned that she may not be returning. That gave me anxiety; and life with its consequences has come again to myself. I cannot escape medical diseases with soul mates. Alison must be quite ill; and it will require months for her to recover because she mentioned that they attacked the recurrent tumor with all the potent chemotherapy drugs and radiation. I feel saddened; but will deal. I am almost crying again as I put the kids down, tuck them in, pray, and read Goodnight Mr. Moon.

Jaiden's croup was improving with steroids and albuterol inhalation treatment. My English class today was discussing fundamentals of using short expressive sentences with proper grammar – including commas, semi-colons, and capitalizing where necessary. I want our students to wince when they view an email or reading with incorrect syntax, spelling, or grammar. I am having our students post their writings and be as proficient as Shakespeare – whether it is a message, short story, or poem. The ability to speak, write, and communicate is ebbing into a lost art with artificial intelligence and IT crafted writings. A term paper may require a couple minutes on AI instead of the required hours of self-research and proper writing. I am demanding that all students place their writings on the computer and classroom site. Additionally, all writings must be duplicated in cursive. I do hear grumbling; but I have parents, students, and associate teachers that are championing our class for fundamentals. I love English and literature; and we are educating an entire class with life skills necessary to compete in the job world via proper communication in speech and writing.

I am attending a birthday party tonight for Josh's class. Many parents are involved with the hats, banners, food, and cake. I went on Amazon and picked a few birthday gifts for many of these birthday parties to stay ahead of the kid birthday party schemes. The birthday games are well planned; and Josh is looking forward to the evening with the entire class. The class has worked hard and has passed the Iowa test skills for their age and beyond. The homework has been steep; but he loves school and is performing well (Janae (my deceased wife) would love that). One of the gals at the party tried to "hit" on me – for lack of a better term. Open flirting with the coach at a kid's birthday party is borderline acceptable behavior. Her name was Mandy; and she was cute. I surmised that she was a single Mom; but who knows? She wanted to talk football; so, I did speak with her about our now popular 2 QB backfield set. Her child has autism; but is performing well in Josh's class. Somehow, I feel autism is over-diagnosed; but I am 100% for treatment to improve a child's education and future plight in life. Mandy somewhat expected a date or rendezvous after the party. I do not need any more girl issues on my plate. In retrospect, I understand that life without a partner is uphill (I am there). There are, however, many issues with 2nd marriages and relationships that involve money, family, and other issues that had not surface during courtship. I am just not ready for serious relationship stuff at present.

We had Saturday morning hoops and then I took our nanny home because her car was not working well. These college girls (the nanny and sub-nanny) are excellent. I am so fortunate; but how long this will continue is beyond my control. The nannies treat our kids so well; and our kids love the nannies. While the kids were playing with the neighborhood kids (including Smitty's kids), a couple well known coaches knocked on the door. I recognized them; and they asked if they could speak "off the record" for a few minutes. They were from an NFL team that was borderline successful the past few years and were searching for some exquisite football coaching skills. Though there has not been a high school coach on record that has entered the NFL without the college experience, I could potentially be the first. I would be an offensive coordinator; and salary would be multiples of my present salary with considerable perks.

The guarantee contract would be 5 years; and all expenses would be paid. I am at a loss; and perhaps Smitty and I could discuss this tonight over a beer. I know he will say: "Go for it." Money and happiness do not necessarily coincide in my mind. The offer was immense; and the reason I dd not have notice by the coaches is because they know I would on the surface say no. They risked their reputations and decorum by just showing up like a missionary. I think about the Indiana State coaches that showed up at Larry Bird's house when he shrugged them away. Larry's Grandma on the front porch in French Lick, Indiana told Larry to listen to the coaches because they mean well and are offering yourself a lifetime of basketball and an education. Bird elected to listen to his grandma; and the rest is history (amazing story).

Day 55

I should not have waited to get our kids enrolled in religious classes. Janae and I had talked about Catholic schools. Living in north Colorado Springs precludes myself from enrolling these kids in Catholic preschool and daily school due to issues with work, nannies, and coaching. We will live with the Sunday morning Catechism instruction at present – barring myself taking a job in Cleveland, Miami, or some other "big-league" metropolis. That was part of the packages that have been offered. I will take advantage of these college and Catholic school offers if I decide to move on (doubtful because it is not Colorado). Smitty seems to think I need to move-on and enjoy my success on a grand scale, sign a long-term guarantee contract, and perhaps return to Colorado later. Who knows what might transpire with a move. Fans, coaches, football media, and the sports world are going crazy over our 2 QB backfield. Obviously, having 2 QBs in the backfield with both being runners and passers creates endless possibilities of offensive schemes, successful trick plays, and keeps defensive coordinators and players on the edge of their careers. I love it.

The media is exposing more of our offense (3 tight end set up with both long and short passing attack). The blocking schemes confuse all defenses; and all defenses are guessing constantly at our offensive schemes and plays. On defense, we blitz nearly continuously; and it can come from a variety of players. Delayed blitzes are my favorite (outside linebacker covering the flat and then sprinting to the opposition QB). Our teams have a defensive gadget with the line backing off at the snap and the 2nd tier of players (safety and linebackers) bull rushing the opposition QB or running back. The mass confusion on blocking schemes by the offense makes total sense. Our goals on defense are to not allow the opposition time to establish blocking schemes with confusing rushes and blitzes. I can diminish the risk of big plays by having speedy secondary players who can cover and close quickly on runners and God – forbid pass catchers. I dream of confusing the defense in every imaginable football manner.

I talked to Alison Simpson DO today. She is a mess with a long recovery ahead; but her spirits were somewhat improved. She is strongly wanting to return to work; but only God knows what will be her fate. None of us know our fate. Nobody knows if they will receive their next breath. I do not feel obligated to now forever be in love with Alison; but even as a friend she will need long-term support. There was never any real commitment by either of us; but my God she is beautiful and a beautiful person.

Day 56

The football world is allover myself with offers, gossip, and social media chatter. I am far more concerned about my English and literature classes, my frosh basketball team, and our kids. The kids have adapted far better than myself to Colorado. Our kids and the neighborhood gang love the hide and seek "KEEN" game where one party is on offense trying to touch the goal before they are tagged. If successful by 100%, they are on offense again. Many squabbles occur whether they touch the tree (home base) before they were tagged. This game carries into the darkness. Coming home it like pulling teeth since none of the kids want to quit. The only reward for coming home is ice cream and a read of Goodnight Mr. Moon. Money cannot purchase this fun for our kids. Jaiden (who can barely walk) plays along with a pass after just learning to walk – but he "gets it."

The English and Literature Class has been rated the best and most difficult in Colorado Sports Academy High School. The parents grin as I discuss the class at parent – teacher conferences. I have heard "old-school" a few hundred times. I

64

love it! When I witness the progress, creativity, work ethic when all these kids are in sports (synergistic), I feel we are winning and preparing student athletes for life and its consequences. There needs to be some discipline within our school; and out English and Literature Class has kept our class working hard in the evenings and weekends. I always inform them they will receive college credit for our class; and other college classes will be easier. Few complaints have occurred due to my praising the writings, reading, spelling, and speech. I am receiving a ton of great feedback from our classes in English and Literature. We are finally done with Shakespeare (for a period).

Missy Bradford called and essentially wanted a date. She was invited to a Denver Nugget party. She needs an escort. I am at a loss of what to say; so, I kindly retort that I will get back to her shortly depending on my schedule. It would be cool to have some contact with a Denver professional basketball team – especially since I am now coaching 70 frosh guys. Missy was very appreciative; and I can discern she is quite interested in myself with all the baggage (3 kids). Thus, most probably without consulting Smitty, I will probably accept. I am not tied down to Alison Simpson; and she may never return to Colorado Springs (or even live). I need to move on with my life and have a ton of decisions to make prior to the next football season.

Janae's parents have read all the mush in the newspapers and social media – threatening to have me removed from Colorado with other football jobs and money. I am sure Sherry and Herb Tompkins will have advice for myself; and I feel as grandparents, they should have some say about visiting their grandkids. The only aspect they do not love is me attached to a Greenwood Village debutante. I can deal with all that chatter and the grandparents – if it does not interfere with coaching and my English and Literature classes. I will always move on and just do the best for myself. A recent book about "Boundaries" was given to me by a student surprisingly. The book's theme is that one needs to take care of his or herself prior to taking care of others. Setting boundaries where others intrude unmercifully of via intruding into one's life is not warranted. Thus, implicitly, or explicitly, the intruder needs to get the message regarding the boundaries you have constructed surrounding yourself (an emotional moat). I need to do what is best for myself, and my kids – others do not matter. Boundaries are established for a reason; and I am not intruding into their lives. There is no preemptive right because I am a coach, teacher, eligible widower, or any other factor that should allow others to penetrate my shield. Goodnight Mr. Moon, Good night kids.

Day 57

Coach Wilford Tremby fortunately or unfortunately made the feature section of the main Denver newspaper on Sunday. Missy Bradford did not write the article; nor did she know about the upcoming feature story. I was stunned when I heard about the story and read the story on-line. Smitty saw the printed article and was in our back-door immediately after the kids had arisen. I am finding a way to get our kids to catechism – church school at the local Catholic Church. The kids look forward and we finished their church homework last evening. There are questions of my faith because of what happened to Janae – Janae's life removed from her while a young mother. The entire metastatic breast cancer aggression at any age before screening was recommended has humbled myself and all her physicians in Chicago. The doctors threw the works at Janae; but nothing worked. And all the therapy appeared to make her condition worse. The pain and screaming were intolerable; and with kids surrounding the home hospice situation, it was pure hell. We have moved on as a family.

While at church some new acquaintances surrounded me after mass when I was picking up the kids. Many parishioners asked about the article and its contents. Few realized that Janae had died early from breast cancer, that we had 3 kids, and that I was coaching frosh basketball for Colorado Sports Academy High School. Surrounded by a group of guys talking football while waiting for catechism to end, a "pushy" young Mom mentioned that she would like me to meet her "single" sister. A couple of the other guys mentioned she was cute and a good catch. I just kept quiet and felt like my privacy was a touch invaded. People mean well; but I can care for myself and my personal relationships. I under-reacted as the nosy church – mom kept harping about her single sister. Many want to play match-makers; but I have a ton on my plate today. The "date" with Missy Bradford is later this afternoon – going to a Nuggets party in Castle Rock – where many Nuggets live.

I survived the crowd surrounding the Catechism. Sherry and Herb Tompkins arrived at our house early and were somewhat upset with my date with Missy Bradford and had many questions about Dr. Alison Simpson – who they preferred. We talked about school, church, the frosh basketball team I am coaching, and my work schedule. The conversation rotated to my college football offers; and potentially moving away from Colorado. They discussed that money was not everything in life and offered to assist with any expenses. I mentioned that I was taking all the information into account; and would do the best for my family. Nothing regarding moves has been decided; and the offers keep coming. The situation is fluid; but I will keep them informed. The kids were quite happy to see their grandparents from Greenwood Village in Denver. The presents bestowed upon the kids were fantastic; and I am comfortable leaving the kids with family. The date with Missy Bradford was shortened because she had several sports stories later that evening. We met at the Denver Nuggets party; and I was able to meet some Nugget players and coaches. The food was terrific; and since I was driving, I could not drink more than a beer. Missy and I hit it off well; and neither party was pushy regarding a "next" date. A couple basketball players read the Denver newspaper article that was published about myself this morning. They had a myriad questions regarding the 2 QB scheme. As I discussed the play schemes, a Denver Bronco coach overheard much of the chatter. He introduced himself after the Nugget players left. He mentioned that Denver is interested in my coaching acumen. I left shocked; and many thoughts raced through my minds as I drove back home on I 25. I need to let life come to me; which it is doing. Enjoy the ride and my family – especially at these young ages.

Day 58

The 2 QB scheme has caught quite the interest – with some of the plays being shown on national sports broadcasts. I thought our defensive blitzing schemes were more innovative than the 2 QB offensive set. I am receiving a myriad of texts, phone calls, and letters regarding my availability – being termed an offensive football genius and many other lofty accolades. I know I am just a reasonably good high school football coach who made his mark by fooling opposition. The large offer from the SEC college team still stands; but they have been good regarding not being too pushy and demanding an answer. They came to me and I only replied that I would consider. Money forever with kids' college and expenses as early adults would not be an issue. I am starting to "settle – in" within Colorado. If I choose not to take a bigger sports job I may regret it years later. Our kids are quite happy, settled, and finally beginning not to ask repeatedly about "mommy." A new mom could enter the picture; but let us wait on life.

I returned to school and am facing an unusual situation in the classroom. The minority students are claiming that there are not enough "minority" writings – especially after Shakespeare study. Colorado Sports Academy High School addressed this with myself. I mentioned that I would bring in readings and translations from the best Hispanic and African American writers – including Alex Haley. Haley was a Pulitzer Prize winner for Malcolm X biography and bringing Americans together through the fictional drama (Roots) in 1977 – tracing back his family for 7 generations. Our class will read both books, perform book reports and watch the Roots drama in class (lengthy). The administration mentioned that should solve all issues with a "white-only" basis for English and literature. I have watched Roots and Malcom X movies and features. The Black studies are excellent; and our class will be rejuvenated by having the experience. Haley brought to light many African American family issues through the books and screen productions. He was an amazing writer.

Missy Bradford called and wanted to "go-out" for a beer on Friday night. I mentioned that I had games until 10 PM with the nanny staying late. I offered her to come to our house late and she accepted – since I need to get the nanny or baby sitter home as quickly as possible. Missy is obviously super-interested in myself; and it may be time for me to plunge into a relationship. I need to think. Goodnight.

Day 59

I awoke and obtained a stern conversation from a dad whose son in 4th string on our basketball squad. Louis is a transfer student this semester and is performing well in school. He has not played much hoops prior; thus, I am teaching him considerable. Dad obviously wants him on the first string. We discussed Louis's strengths and weaknesses. I reminded his dad that high school hoops is competition; and not participation. I also mentioned that if we cut the team at 13 players, he might be in a mall. I am giving his son a major chance to play endless hoops; and want him to learn the sport for life. He may never play a varsity game;

but at least this year he will know where he stands regarding his peers and the depth chart. Dad is highly interested; and I discussed that 1 child in 10 million starts on an NBA team. The goal with basketball is discipline, fitness, teamwork, and learning the sport for life. Dad felt good after the discussion. I do not mind dealing with parents – fully understanding where their child interests lie. A large percentage of dads in our society are not involved with their kids; and I would rather have dad involved than not involved. I also discussed not having a driveway hoop meant the family was not serious about basketball – because shooting hoops daily is required for the skill of basketball. Michael Jordan shot buckets before sunrise; but his neighbors did not mind because he was Michael Jordan.

The class loves the Roots story; and other Colorado Sports Academy High School instructors are adopting it for their classrooms. Roots is an American Classic; and there has been nothing similar and as intense as what Roots exposed – from the original slave stealing to how well many slaves were treated and some emancipated. American history has its ugly moments; and Roots exposed the good and bad of the culture as we witnessed 7 generations of Alex Haley's family. Though some of this was fictional; the ideas expressed made strong impressions on all the students. Considerable discussion was generated from the book and television drama we played in class. I felt Roots depicted society for many years in America (before our nation became a county and beyond). I love history amidst my English and Literature classes.

Jaiden had an earache and recurrent otitis media (middle ear infection). The sub pediatrician for Alison Simpson DO mentioned that it did not appear that Alison would be returning to work at the pediatric clinic. Alison instructed myself that she did not want me calling or contacting her until she was better. Since I have not heard from her, I am assuming she is not in good health. She may be under considerable chemotherapy and having other treatments (immunotherapy). I feel that I should call or email; but I respect her condition. The sub pediatrician (who now may be the regular pediatrician), did a wonderful job on Jaiden's ear pain and infection. Despite the tonsils and adenoids gone; the ear aches and infections have returned. We may need an allergist; but for now, the antibiotics have worked wonders. The phone rings after I tucked the kids into bed with Goodnight Mr. Moon. On the phone is Alison Simpson, possibly my girlfriend. I will be supportive and deal!

Day 60

Alison struggled to talk for about 20 minutes – stating she is at the Mayo Clinic in Rochester, Minnesota receiving complex chemotherapy. Her weakness, pallor, malaise, and fatigue as she describes are all self-evident. Advanced leukemia is surging; and her bone marrow was replaced with drug elimination and now a transplant from a relative donor. She is in miserable condition; and it readily shows through her weak voice. I offered a visit; and she says to remember the good times we shared; and there is not much hope for her. I talked to her mother who concurred. Alison appeared healthy, skied, and was a bright light at the parties. Alison was an excellent pediatrician and socially intriguing. I am at a loss for words; but knew enough from Janae to not sit still and offer support in any way possible. Alison wished she had told me about the disease before we had a few dates. She mentioned that she resigned her position as it is unlikely she will return to work or viable life. I am just blown away at the circumstances; and now understand why everyone at the pediatric clinic looked down and depressed when her name was mentioned. I will have to deal with the circumstances; and it will be a "thing" on local social media undoubtedly. Herb and Sherry Tompkins (former in-laws in Greenfield Village (Denver)), will bring this to me. I cannot wait.

The Sporting News and some other publications want some play diagrams in their magazines. I offered to place these in coaching manuals and sports' fans publications that are on line and in paper. I did not want to give away all the plays; but it appears what I do not provide will be improvised. On defense, the alternating and confusing blitzes come from all angles, require practice, and is very confusing to the offense. We have an "All-Out" Blitz that resembles a Tsunami; and variations that reduce the blitz to one person – where the play {based on scouting} is most probably our defense will confront. The defense has to more than match-up. A solid defense must not only win against the block, but be able to shed the block and make the tackle or stuff the run – allowing teammates to close. Man advantages on defense are critical as one play can decide a game. I do believe that most football people are interested in our offensive schemes to obtain advantages and scoring.

Our 2 QB set (not always utilized) sets the dominant QB behind center or off to the side (where either back can receive a lateral snap). The lateral snap requires substantial practice and coordination based on reps and proper numbering systems – with the line and skill players all understanding where the play and its offensive advantages are attacking. The 2 QB set allows both QBs to pass and run, option, and handoff with reverses to one another for passes downfield or back to each other. Defenses are fortunate a when they obtain a no-gain or loss. Overwhelming defensive power and athletic advantages will surpass the offense occasionally, the 2 QB set must have the most athletic, strong, and field aware-ness football players in these positions. I do platoon the 2 QB set; and we do run conventional plays with 1 QB offensive schemes. The second QB can function as a wide-out, halfback, or flanker. When walking up to the line of scrimmage we note feat in the defense, we have an advantage on the play before the snap. This will bring more coaching offers – many of which I am reviewing this afternoon while the kids are outside in the neighborhood.

Day 61

The kids are having so much fun outside playing in this neighborhood. The games are continuous; and I feel like playing some evenings. I wonder what the kids would think if they knew we had an upcoming move to a larger city with a college or professional team. They would not be happy; but they would be accepting overall. The friendships at this age are fluid and not cemented when they become high school students (a very difficult move). Society is so mobile; and all jobs (not just football) are accepting of short tenures and moving to accommodate what is best for the individual and family. It is such that no job is secure; so, a coach or anyone else must always be looking up for the best opportunity. In my profession, locker or classroom accusations may occur. The guilty until proved innocence is the model. Sadly, the Denver coach who we nearly hired went through hell to accomplish his name clearing. He is forever scarred; and I do not know if he returned to coaching. I truly felt sorrow for this guy who had a stellar coaching record in Denver high schools. It required only a girl to falsely accuse him of sexual impropriety as a teacher and coach to ruin his career. And unfortunately, the claimant walks away without recourse. There are risks with every profession.

The school is buzzing with many classmates wanting into our English and Literature classes. We are studying various ethnic writers and are dwelling on "Roots" by Alex Haley. Many questions of ethics of slavery and the causes and perpetuation have occurred. Modernly, it is tough to describe that slavery existed within our system; and how the founders dealt with that in apportioning house votes (the 3/5 rule for slaves – noting 2 % of slaves were white, 1% Indian, and 97^ Black). Freedom came from masters selling slaves into freedom – generally from Northern states. The Emancipation in all ways from slavery and poverty for all ethnicities is still ongoing; and will never end. Our capitalistic system of economics has winners and losers; but we all have a responsibility to treat impoverished families with support. The bible unmistakably states that we will be judged based on how we treat disadvantaged families. The English and Literature Class at Colorado Sports Academy High School has been enlightened by the story of Roots – though it has some fictional qualities in its final prose and film. I could watch and read the episodes repeatedly.

Sherry Tompkins (Janae's mom) calls and wants details on Alison Simpson. Thus, I inform her of the misfortune and inform her of the periodic dates with Missy Bradford. Herb and Sherry Tompkins are inviting me again to their house for a coming out of the Greenfield Village eligible gals. This is a floating quarterly party that attracts younger and elder people of money and fame. I grudgingly accept the offer; and Sherry says I might be surprised at the young gals attending. She has accepted to a degree that I am my own person and do know how to pick a mate. I wonder with Janae picking me how she felt. The Tompkins certainly love the grandkids; and have been very supportive with babysitting at the last minute. Janae's respect demands that I respect the grandchildren family involvement and interactions. I talk to my Life Coach (NP Sally Swift) weekly; and she says go to the mini "coming – out" party at the in-laws. I might be surprised! I am off to sleep!

Day 62

My life coach suggested I concentrate on my kids, teaching, and coaching. It is obvious that these gals are on the rebound and need a relationship – even if not perfect. Love can be transcendent and fleeting. A few months after you are married and possibly onto more offspring, troubles can erupt. I was so in love in round 1 that round 2 may never add up to round 1. That is my biggest fear; so according to the life coach, I need to be picky (as should the girl). Few mature adults at this stage are looking for a short relationship or an escort to a ski party. They are thinking long term commitments. I am therefore stuck in having to sort things out with gals that are providing an excellent initial presentation (akin to a job interview – it is a marriage interview). If things are not what I want in

71

a long-term relationship, I need to part ways (difficult, but necessary). Though we all can marry many varying opposite sex people, I will chance that the right person will hit me in the face (as Janae did in round 1). I need to do what is best for me; and not feel sorry or obligated to someone I have no interest in a long-term relationship. This stuff is tough; and though it would be nice to a mom for the kids – it is not a necessity.

The athletic director position was insidiously relegated to another administrative coach during football season – as we advanced through the playoffs the super-intendent did not want to disrupt me from coaching and teaching duties. My salary remained the same (small increase). And my endless hassles dealing with parents, transgender locker room stuff, drug and alcohol issues (though few), inequitable playing time, and the uncommon racial complaint have left my desk. I am into teaching English and literature with coaching football. Though I am coaching frosh boys' hoops, I do not feel the pressure of a 5A football program maintaining its stature. I love the hoops coaching; and our teams have incurred success and immense growth. The student athletes have been fabulous; and I know that most will play hoops the rest of their lives in some capacity. Some of our team will play college (probably D2 or D3).

The kids are doing well in school (Josh and Jake); while Jaiden is growing with his very own personality. The "mom" banter has quieted; so, perhaps we do not need a real mom if that does not enter my life. Sally Swift, the NP life coach, has directed my to not just go on dates; but make conscious efforts to envision yourself down the road with the dated gal as a life-long partner. I narrated that I would do the best job I could – spending time with an individual makes sense – but there is also a pseudo form of commitment occurring. This is so much more difficult than round 1. I will just deal.

Day 63

Dr. Alison Maples (my pediatrician girlfriend who I have seen for weeks) called from the Mayo Clinic. She was nice, friendly, and sincere. Her honesty was amaz-ing as she relayed that her leukemia treatment was not working well, exhaustion was immense, and she retired from her pediatric practice in Colorado Springs. Though she might return, Alison was mainly concerned about living. She mentioned that she missed me; and how much I meant to her. She understood what becoming a permanent partner meant with my kids. At present, she readily admitted her body could not handle three small kids (barring recovery). It was wonderful to talk to her; and I am at a loss as to the next step. Alison did not say move on with other relationships; but implied by her words and demeanor that she was not a long-term partner. I cried a small amount since I know what she has been dealing with (like Janae incurred for many weeks). There are just some diseases that cannot be arrested; and I have had strong relationships with two women that were so unfortunate. I queried traveling and visiting Alison; howev-er, she stated that she was in poor medical health clinically. Visiting would not be a great idea since the disease and treatment have taken their toll immensely (lost weight, pallor, anemia, fatigue, and muscle wasting).

The endless offers from college and now pro sports teams are in fluxing my mailbox and email. I am not certain of the next step since things are going well in Colorado. I have seen my name attached to the double QB set on some of the sports and football talk shows on radio, television, and internet. The comments have been mostly positive. A few sports pundits and coaches mention injuries to a second-string QB could be fatal to a competitive football team. I say phooey - because I would rather risk injury and win games than lose and have an excellent football back that can pass sitting on the bench all season. I expect both QBs to run; and in all leagues quarterbacks have running plays. Some teams are now experimenting with the 2 QB offensive set in the off-season with success. All teams have a qualified 3rd string QB – who I would not hesitate to place in the backfield. Interestingly, the Denver Broncos (not far from our house) are experimenting with the 2 QB offensive set. The advantages in play scheming and misdirect are immense. The defenses we played against using pro and wishbone offensive sets with 2 QBs in the backfield left the game dumbfounded. Generally, Colorado Sports Academy High School has now been placed on the map. Football players are wanting to play at our school – with the caveat of being a good student (required).

Smitty stopped by for a beer and discussed the neighborhood, his passing romance with an office girl in his IT office, and his lawyer dealing with his former wife wanting custody of his kids (though she is insane and still in an asylum or state hospital). Smitty has been depressed; but is fighting so his kids do not have to deal with a severe bipolar mom the rest of their childhood. There is no person on our planet without some strong issues. We all just deal with life's successes and low points. It is great our kids are playing together well. Spark, our new family dog, fits in well playing kids games. I am very fortunate to have a great kids' neighborhood. Janae would have loved our neighbors and the surrounding kid environment. Perhaps she is watching. Smitty wants to discuss basketball plays; and how our frosh boys basketball team needs to press 24/7. I love it!

Day 64

My day is busy with nannies because the regular nanny became ill. The sub nanny was out of town; so, I used Smitty's nanny. The neighbors were more than happy to help as we have had some social interactions on back decks in the neighborhood. Janae would have loved this Colorado community. Again, I need to move on with my life. I keep grinding backwards over my wife. Janae instructed me to write my inner-feelings so the kids can read their dad's diary when they become older. Fake feelings will be detected; but real sentiment will be truly meaningful. I am really beginning to enjoy the diary writing; as it provides a time of reflection. My life coach loves that I am writing down my sensibilities as close to daily as I can muster. Some days and nights I love to write because I am in a writing frame of mind with my deep thoughts ready to be transcribed from my mind onto my computer. I may never reveal the diary until I am on my death doorstep. Our kids may want to review this when I am not so concerned about what the family may think. Presently, there is zero that is shameful within the writings. Life is unpredictable. None of this would have occurred if I had not picked up Janae's coat that caught the turnstile at Chicago's Soldier Field. Amazing how she found me with my Manion High School Coaches Jacket insignia and probably no wedding ring (I am told gals review the hand prior to becoming interested). Janae admitted this to me later. All romances have a differing beginning; and serendipity is more common than uncommon in the union of male and female.

I have had to field complaints from the English and Literature class that we are too much into college level studies, excessive homework, and how is helping my future life. I informed the class and administration that I was preparing them for life as a business person in Hong Kong, communicating with a business over your plumbing contract, or yourself teaching 5th grade in Denver. The English and literature skills with phonics are critical to your future. Personal interaction, writing, and presentation of yourself in a relationship as a teacher, coach, parent, business partner, or engaging yourself to the opposite sex in a respectful manner is decisive. My bias is that everyone belongs in my class and should obtain a minor in English – be it trade school or college. I am always available by phone or internet if a student struggles. Colorado Sports Academy High School is not just about sports – it is student athletes from trainers to pole vaulters. Our school emphasizes academics. A student here for just football is in the wrong time zone. Our mission at our school is to graduate student athletes with honors – helping them to the next step in life. Colorado Sports Academy High School is not for everyone. High School here is work.

Smitty called and wanted a beer to watch some hoops at his house with a brew. The kids were wide awake and had their homework completed. Thus, I treaded over to the neighbor Smitty's house with some appetizers. We diagrammed some plays on the kids' chalkboard; and I walked away with a different scheme off our standard 131 trapping zone press. The zone tightens when the ball comes to the corners or sides; however, I noted that bringing our deep cover #5 man up and veering toward the obvious throw – risking a deep pass and layup – may invite turnovers by the opposition. Presses are difficult if performed correctly. The offense is required to work double to score; however, the drain on our resources without a great bench is risky. Rick Pitino's "94 Feet of Hell" wins basketball games. Smitty should probably be the frosh basketball coach. We discussed all the football offers; and I remarked that I was just trying to get through this season. I am scheduled to coach golf; but with family, kids, need for downtime, and perhaps dating, I may defer that obligation. I am dreading this Sunday's social at Jane's parents in Greenwood Village. Sport coat, tie, and shined shoes (the works) is required. The kids are coming also since The Tompkins as grandparents cannot stay away from our kids (I love it)!

Day 65

The day after the last frosh games was exciting. Many parents loved the idea of no cuts and our frosh team with > 50 players all playing. It is beyond intramurals because there is coaching. All the players have hoops in their driveways or access to a nearby basketball court. Grades are rising from our mandates – you cannot be on the team if you are less than a B average. Academics are the #1 focus; and thinking I am NBA material and do not need the education is a sin. I talk endlessly that NBA players with education have better court vision, know when to rest, understand their "go to" strengths, and work on weaknesses. Education makes basketball players adept and quick on their feet. Education is a life-long pursuit in all professions. I want the very best in all my players – whether they score 1 point or 30 points in a basketball contest. Ball skills are learned by having a basketball in your hands 24/7; or when not in school of sleeping. Many great ballers slept with a basketball.

The" coming – out" party Sunday afternoon at Janae's parents in Greenfield Village within Denver was interesting. The three kids (Josh, Jake, and Jaiden) had friends outside for play. The number of people from the upper echelon of Denver society was incredible (> 100). Everyone was dressed, the food was great, and I met many interesting people from all professions – including IT company CEOs, sports media, and wealthy neighbors. The Tompkins (Janae's parents) ensured I met every eligible gal and their parents – many coming as a family. One gal who was shy caught my eye (Mandy Sagan). She was a friendly reserved 20-Some-thing, gorgeous blue-eyed blonde with a killer smile. Mandy was the Bronco cheerleader player coach. Her main job was ICU Nursing with a doctorate degree and head nurse position in a south Denver hospital. We conversed loosely; and her family chimed in about my football coaching. They knew we won the Illinois 5A Championship last year. They loved our football team story with an upstart (Colorado Sports Academy High School) capturing the Colorado 5A High School Championship this year. Mandy's dad was a tremendous multi-sports player and fan. Both parents were nice; and Mandy's brother was exceedingly friendly.

Though Mandy was shy, she followed me around from a short distance and smiled frequently. Is that flirting? I do not know. And everyone at this Sunday social knew of my situation with three small kids and widower status (Janae's parent ensured everyone attending knew beforehand). I do not think I am a good catch with three small kids (ages 6,4, and nearly 2). Perhaps there is some looks, structure, and character within me; but why would a gal want to inherit and be a step mom to 3 little kids. Love trumps all else; and initial appearances send sig-nals between males and females. There were signals transferring between Mandy and myself. She is gorgeous, athletic, the right age, and apparently her family has dollars. I am a middle-class teacher and coach. There is wide socio-economic separation with me and everyone in this lush neighborhood of Greenfield Vil-lage. Janae obviously married down in socio-economic spheres; so, I am certain Sherry and Herb Tompkins informed everyone that somehow, they are my sponsors. I left the Sunday social with the kids late after talking to Mandy for an hour as everyone left. Why is Mandy not married or bringing a boyfriend to the occasion? I wonder if there were drugs, divorce(s), mental disease (she seemed shy but normal), or gay? I am certain Janae's mom will know the neighborhood scoop. I am rushing to escape the typical storm in Larkspur with its golf ball size hail. Today was a grind; but overall, very good. I am glad I went to the Sunday social at Grandma's house.

75

Day 66

Today, I received a call from a parent on the frosh basketball team. The mom stated her son was ingesting illicit drugs including fentanyl, cocaine, amphetamines, THC, and kratom. I asked how he was staying alive; and she responded that he has been in the ER twice with prolonged observation and detoxification. He is severely addicted and will probably die without treatment. She felt that basketball would potentially save him. I was shocked and dismayed that the student athlete had said nothing to the coaching staff about the drugs. Our team policy is to suspend for a week; and then dismiss from the team for adverse team behavior. The mom felt the basketball player would kill himself if he was released or suspended from the team. I took mom's contact information down and said we would discuss this with the coaches and AD. I am certain I will receive a near unanimity opinion regarding releasing him from the team. Deep inside, we all know this is not the best way to treat him. The mother wanted the son admitted to a drug rehabilitation center; but he refused. The dad has left the marriage and a divorce is shortcoming. Mom has 3 other children – who are behaving well. My comments regarding dad stepping up and helping remain restrained. This is our society modernly – at least a substantial minority. I vowed to help this player in some manner. I will bring him into my office tomorrow; and we will talk.

Every issue on an athletic team needs to be handled individually. There are some ground rules; and out freshman player has broken many. I will inform the coaching staff and the AD of the issues; and inform them of my wish for a short suspension, drug treatment ongoing, and maintaining a B average. I will inform mom of the battle plan. We all have issues; but these are serious. I will offer my treatment plan and state that our player (who has been moving up on the depth chart), needs to step up and obtain treatment or suffer the ill consequences of disease and potential death. This will not be easy.

As I was driving home, the gal I met at the Tompkins Sunday social (Mandy) texted me and wanted to talk. I called her back and she was very nice and invited me to another social gathering at the Denver Jewish Community Center Saturday evening. The play is the history of Stephen Sondheim, the father of Broadway. Sondheim's biggest hit was West Side Story's music. Sondheim is my favorite; and the most beloved of all Broadway musical librettists. I said yes and Mandy stated she would meet me there or I could escort her with her providing me with the appropriate address (next to Janae's parents – who probably have something to do with this date). Yes, this is a real date. The play is 2.5 hours and ends at 2030. I texted Mandy and stated I would pick her up at 5 PM. I asked if she would like to eat something before or after the musical. She invited me over to her house and I accepted – stating it would be dessert. What am I getting into again? It is time to talk to Smitty. Where is Janae when I need her?

Day 67

The kids absolutely love Monument, Colorado. They are performing well in school, have gobs of friends, have a nice puppy named Spark, and now only oc-casionally talk about mom. I will get through this and review this in years ahead as a sign of strength and resilience – but it is tough. The stories at night, birthday parties, skiing, and overall family enmeshment into the community has grown. The offers from colleges and some professional teams including Spring profes-sional football (the UFL) have continued to grow. The money from the one SEC school is immense; and I would be set for life by accepting the offer. Money is not everything; but I have come to grasp that it is necessary for growth, investment, kids, college, retirement, and overall life's needs. I am not guaranteed a position at Colorado Sports Academy High School – we have one-year contractual terms. Nothing is guaranteed in life. I discovered that with Janae's illness. Now my three kids have a family; and I am the pillar for life. I need to make decisions based on what is best for my kids. Moving them into another city would be brutal; but they are young enough to withstand a new environment – unlike teens. My peers at Colorado Sports Academy High School know of my predicament and a boatload of opportunities with both the Illinois and Colorado State 5A football champion-ships won the past two years.

I have received a lucrative offer to begin a podcast of football plays. I am consid-ering it; and Smitty has given me the thumbs up. It would be a simple podcast of football plays with the label: "My Playbook" by Coach Wilford Tremby. Specific features would be labeled: "First and Goal," "Depth Chart," and "2-Minute Drill." The sports media has gone crazy over our 2-Quarterbacks in the backfield. Wild-cat QB runs, side snaps to a passer, laterals followed by pass/run options have created havoc for our opponents (I love it). Soon, teams will catch us; and I will need to be more creative offensively. The 2 – QB setup is termed:" 2-QB set". All plays off this standard pro-set include run/pass options and trickery. One of my favorite plays is the bootleg sprint option. If the outside linebacker or defen-sive end has the play contained, a simple optional flip of the ball to an opposite running QB allows not just a running opportunity, but downfield passing with appropriate blocking is repeatedly open. Two strong arms in the backfield with the 2 QB set is now being discussed at all levels of football. I love it; and it may make me some lifelong income. The media is calling it the "Tremby" offense.

Smitty thinks Mandy is the real deal. He has already checked her out on social media; and she is clean (no drugs, dumps, psychiatric admissions, lost kids, or diseases). Smitty thinks this is a good match because she has already seen my kids and knows what she is potentially dealing with (a widower with three little kids). Smitty feels it is cool she invited you to her house on Day 1. I am not certain what this means; but my life coach (Sandy Swift – NP psychologist) feels I need to go with these nice potential relationships. I am a touch excited about this gal; but we will determine where this is going after Saturday evening. Time for bed!

Day 68

An article in a national sports publication was released today about Wilford Tremby's 2 – QB set offensive attack. The sports writer termed the offense: "The Ambush." I am receiving notoriety; yet, the writers have not witnessed us play or viewed the playbook (I will never promote our playbook float in public). The assistant coaches, players, AD, and fans love the 2-QB set – call it "The Ambush" – or any sports term you desire. The social media surrounding the article has my email box and ancillary Twitter, Facebook, Linked-In, and other IT communications flooded. High School plays that were successful towards the end of the season when we introduced the 2 QB set in the backfield are now all over the globe. I have players wanting try-outs. I have received everything from more job offers to marriage proposals (sight unseen). I do not know what to discern from hundreds of comments, offers, and coaches wanting to purchase the playbook. The national podcaster wants a contractual deal that will pay me substantially because his site is supported by advertising. I will promote the site just by talking football. I am not certain what I should be doing if anything. There is a ton on my plate; and my three boys are understandably my main concern.

I will not sleep for a couple nights – wondering if I should accept a football job far away from Colorado that allows me to essentially have my financial life secure. There are serious nice girls I could bunk with and the kids have a "real" mom. Then, there would be more pregnancies, blending of step kids, and onward to complexities of life. Perhaps I was destined to be a widower. You cannot really date without the intention of moving the relationship forward – meaning a Super Bowl win (marriage). I can talk to Smitty down the block and my life coach forever and not come up with an answer. The general answer if you do not know what to do is to "stay-put." I also have a career; and I could be fired over a misguided student accusation, bad season, or school board dislike. Church, God, prayers, and my surroundings will provide guidance to my future life. I am on-board with nothing but good options. People in the neighborhood, school, church, and public have been extremely nice to our family since moving. I would hate to leave north Colorado Springs. I am still thinking.

The date with Mandy is set for Saturday evening; and many guys like myself are woefully unprepared. I need to purchase some semiformal clothes, a gift for the gal (possibly flowers), and purchase new cologne off Amazon – that is easy. There are multiple critical steps in dating; plus, I need to get a baby-sitter. Josh says I am dating a potential new "mom." That is probably true; but I do not want to admit such things. I am a little nervous because I do like this gal – even though she is from Janae's parent neighborhood. I do like her; and cannot worry about Alison or Missy; nor anyone else. The encounter was another serendipity because I did not want to attend Janae's mother social mini-debutante social gathering on a Sunday afternoon. Leaving the kids requires dress, nanny, kid's meals plans and homework complete, and dealing with Spark, the dog. I am going to bed – wish me luck.

Day 69

Today, I dealt with a ton from the student who overdosed. He finally admitted to a continuous flow of drugs, sales to support his drug habit, and other illicit behavior. We spent 90 minutes of my "teacher" time devoted to his miscues. I informed him of the policy; and rightfully he should be permanently suspended. In summary, his behavior was in part emanating from his parents' ensuing divorce, not seeing his dad because he moved out of state, and break-up with a girlfriend. As coach and now father, I steered this student athlete into the ultimate "Land of Oz" if he improved with his deportment, grades, and became drug free. His suspension was one-week, a minimum B average was required on all tests and grades, and any illicit drugs or behavior would result in suspension for the basketball season. I will counsel him weekly; and the coaches, AD, and administration are all on-board with the treatment. We cannot cure the family situation. The kid needs a dad badly; and now wants me to be his dad. The mom is super-cute; however, that is only within my "guy" mind. She could potentially be a surface to air missile within a relationship. The mom will have a difficult time finding a new partner potentially because of her son's behavior – who would want to engender this mess at home for years. Lust, relationships, romance, and family life are balanced by arrests, jail, drug treatment centers, and failure to ever launch. Colorado is stuffed with kids on the fence of life who are in their parents' basement smoking pot 24/7.

Our team has had discussions from medical personnel and career professionals. Basically, THC lowers a student's IQ 15-20 points and can result in dementia if smoked endlessly. Promoted as a cure-all for everything, marijuana becomes a modality of behavior encompassing your life – physically and psychologically addicting. THC has taken Colorado by storm; and is winning. The suspended student asked about THC use as a medication; and I said the Colorado Sports Academy High School can drug test. If a student athlete tests positive for THC, then they are suspended from the team. We are not allowing medical personnel to invoke or write "fake" scripts stating these students need this drug. Sorry, I told him-this is our drug policy (like alcohol with underage drinking). The talk went well; and I do feel this kid (Herby Smith) will respond positively. Herby Smith is moving up the depth charts in basketball – playing well in scrimmages and practices – how he does that with drugs I cannot discern.

The end of our talk with Herby Smith was discussing the baseline "Indiana" cut. There are variations of the cut beginning with a quick L cut to receive the ball in the lane and use a quick step back shot, baby hook, or drive with a reverse. If the defender is screened, the ball goes up immediately. If tight defense, then the baby hook, reverse, pivot, or pass out of the play is required. My favorite is to butt the defender near the basket after receiving an unexpected pass and self – cut with a dribble towards the basket for a jump stop or layup. If the defender is close, continue offensively to score and obtain an "And – One." Practice with scrimmages and individual moves perfected in pick-up are needed. The Indiana cut move does not just happen. I left the meeting with Herby discussing the play in detail with a clipboard. I am not only his coach; I am his new dad.

Day 70

The date with Mandy went exceptionally well. We had lunch at her house – well prepared. She lives down the block from Herb and Shelly Tompkins (Janae's parents). I know they had something to do with this now known assignation. Mandy Sagan is Ashkenazi Jewish, has gorgeous brown eyes and dark hair with a broad nose. Mandy was married for a few months and obtained a civil annulment. I am now Catholic; and Mandy knew more about me than I know about myself. Surprisingly, when we talked openly, she knew I was coming to the semi-formal Sunday afternoon social at the Tompkins, knew I was Catholic, knew Janae well, studied my football records and playbook, and spied all the open internet/social media football coaching offers. Mandy was a captain Bronco cheerleader, ski instructor, prom queen, and was the president of Delta Zeta at Radcliffe College (Harvard's sister school) – the top sorority known for a combination of looks and intelligence. Mandy, despite, the accolades, was well down to earth. She is a finance person for sports organizations such as the Nuggets and Broncos in Denver. She consults with many corporations and individuals regarding everything from real estate investments to taxes. Mandy's first marriage was beset with her husband having unexpected affairs. He married his last affair. This entire sequence sent Mandy into mental decline for months – to considering quitting work, life, and ever having a partner male relationship again.

Mandy's parents and family obviously wanted Jewish; but her last husband was the pick of the litter and failed. She respects her religious legacy and family; but does not own everything (including marriage) that tags along with Jewish tradition (marrying within the religion). I am a football coach and English/literature instructor. Why would she be attracted to me? I am woefully poor considering her family's probable trust, her income, and household in Greenfield Village. Mandy is outgoing; but beyond that, this is on its face not a good match. She knows everyone in Denver and beyond. Mandy knows many NFL and college administrators. Underneath the print and off the playing field, Mandy is critical to the economic financial success of many sports teams. Mandy can calculate in her head how many logo shirts the QB of a team will sell based on the team's records and individual statistics. She became known for popularity through her cheerleading and discussions of financial remuneration with Denver sports teams. The Bronco cheerleading squad financial records were impressive to all of football and many sports organizations. As a cheerleader, the squad was readily at all games, some practices, and many corporate events performing. This activity kept in shape; and shaped her future financial career. Mandy is the complete package. Why me?

The night went well and a repeat date was in order. She had a great mini – supper and dessert at her house after the long Sondheim show. We talked incessantly during breaks as I had our Colorado Sports Academy High School literature classes study Sondheim religiously. Mandy wanted to know all about our kids, friends, neighborhood, and my work (assistant coaches, teachers, and players). She knew I was coaching a frosh basketball squad and wanted to attend some games (really). Mandy was quite open and frankly said she wanted a "real" guy, kids galore, and a positive marriage. I asked again why me? She said it was simple. She knew, respected, and competed against Janae at everything from volleyball to boyfriends. Janae made great decisions in moving to Chicago, latching onto me, and producing great kids. Mandy mentioned that I was on every social media forum with hundreds of young gals wanting a football coach type guy with common sense and killer looks. I was shocked, embarrassed, and overcome. Mandy said the world is ahead of you; and it may not be at Colorado Sports Academy High School. I left with a kiss and a date after the frosh game Wednesday after school – which she will attend. I am flattered!

Smitty stopped over after supper and asked about Mandy. He was reading this on a social media platform that I was spotted at the Sondheim musical with Mandy Sagan. Now Smitty knows more about Mandy Sagan than I do. Smitty now states I have 3 solid girlfriends. Missy Bradford was a short fling, Doctor Alison Maples is possibly dying, and now Mandy Sagan (one date). Smitty and I talk after he lets it be known that his office romance that failed has been reinitiated. Smitty readily admits that this may not last; but it is holding and a life raft is not being thrown overboard. I want the very best for Smitty; and he will obtain a partner relationship and marriage potentially (blended family). Smitty wanted to know more about Mandy beyond the Bronco cheerleader, Radcliffe sorority legacy, ski instructor, and prom queen stuff. Smitty mentioned she was married before and incurred an annulment. Was Mandy grumpy or difficult? Thus, I told Smitty the openness, want of a family, Jewish heritage, and her financial career (MBA at Wharton School of Business in Philadelphia, Pennsylvania after Radcliffe). Smitty was blown away; and said to plan an offensive attack she cannot refuse. Smitty said with my intuitive playbook, a white flag from her could come within 3 months. This is guy talk; and a couple beers exaggerated Smitty's claims. He remains a good friend in guiding my life.

School was intense today with some students struggling over common English grammar including sentence structure, adverbs, adjectives, comma placements, and flow of their writing with paragraphs inciting new ideas. I will be after school and have my assistants run the frosh basketball squad. Many teachers in prior years disregarded common English structure, phonics, and syntax. Learning where and when to capitalize a word is learned in the 4th grade; yet, many intelligent students project inadequate English fundamentals. As English and Literature instructor, I need to clear these hurdles and "make-up" for poor teaching preemptive to our high school class. I love this part of my life because I enjoy and know English and literature. I would hate to retire from teaching and just coach – though I am reviewing some high-profile coaching appointments with long healthy financial incentives. As Mandy stated, the world is in front of myself. I am nervous in a good way.

The kids (Josh, Jake, and Jaiden) after homework and supper put on their swimming suits and traveled to the Woodland Park waterpark pool. This was excellent with a lazy river, water slides, and few people. It was wonderful. I bumped into an assistant basketball coach whom our frosh hoop team scrimmaged. We talked basketball while the kids were swimming and I held Jaiden (kicking). The Woodland Park coach asked which job I was reviewing and potentially grasping. Surprised, I informed him that nothing has been decided; and I may stay at the same job with Colorado Sports Academy High School. He was surprised; and I felt not taking the step into college or pro- ball was a career failure. I am back to the life coach, NP Sandy Swift, for some advice on dealing with social media, dating, and internet chatter. I need to set boundaries, enjoy the ride, be the best parent, and potentially find an appropriate new mom for these kids.

I have embarked in my English, Literature, and Composition class some great writers of the past including my list of Homer from Ancient Greece (The Iliad and Odyssey) and Geoffrey Chaucer's (1343 – 1400) poems have influenced all our writings from England and theatre. John Bunyan's (1628 – 1688) Pilgrim Progress was right behind the bible in sales – discussing religion from a Baptist perspective. Jane Austin (1775 – 1817) and her popularity was right behind Shakespeare with English novels. Hans Christian Anderson (1805-1875) wrote extensively children's stories. Charles Dickens (1812-1870) wrote exquisite novels still commonly read and studied modernly. Herman Melville (1819-1891) wrote Moby Dick. Leo Tolstoy (1828-1910) wrote War and Peace. Emily Dickinson (1830-1886) wrote poetry for the ages; and her sister discovered 2,000 poems after she died. James Joyce (1882-1941) wrote a collection of short stories that are revered in modern literature. F. Scott Fitzgerald wrote The Great Gatsby in his short life (1896-1941). George Orwell (1903-1950) wrote 1984 – still read and influential within literature circles modernly. The student can choose which author, read the manuscript, and file a complete non-AI book report. I love it. This is a semester project; and the class will hopefully thank me in years to come.

Jaiden came down with bronchitis and RSV this morning. I was late to school with a sub teacher fill-in at the last minute thankfully. I went to the new pediatrician and he began antibiotics because of the fever. Steroids, inhalation bronchodilators, and fluids were initiated in the office. We were at the pediatrician's office for 4 hours. I was happy Jaiden was relieved. I am staying home and my assistant coach will coach the frosh hoop squad later today. I can observe my son needing a mom. I am adequate; but not the real deal. Kids need moms and dads. Somehow this is not right. Janae should not have died early from metastatic breast cancer. I am reliving the past and again need to move on. Coaching, teaching, and being a dad and mom are overwhelming. I am on the hot seat with girls, job offers, and the stress of making decisions. I love being busy; but this is inordinate. My life coach, NP and psychologist Sally Swift, seems to think I am fine and going with the flow. I could take a Southeast Conference coaching job tonight – because they are not waiting forever with large amounts of dough. Their football program needs to move on. I need to move on. Perhaps I should not have left Chicago; but Janae's wish that I succeed in Colorado came true. I am in North Colorado Springs because of my former wife.

New recruits for our program keep coming to our school. We have attracted the very best athletes; and should be competitive for the next few years thankfully. I have 5 QBs on the depth chart for next year. They know I will play 3-4 players – with 2 on the field frequently. All QBs have read and understood our Ambush offense. The media has termed this The Carpet-Bombing Attack or Colorado Arsenal. Though the insinuation of killing innocent people and not military structures is immoral; the fans, coaches, and players get the football meaning. I love it because like a hail storm, bombs can emanate from anywhere in our backfield. Carpet-bombing is not a pc term, but I like it. I know history and carpet bombing in World War II killed thousands; so, I will recommend Wilford Tremby's Ambush as our offensive scheme with 2 quarterbacks. Bedtime!

Mandy Sagan called and wanted to know how Jaiden was progressing from his bronchitis and RSV. I wondered how she knew. Apparently, someone in the pediatrics office or another patient jumped on social media and reported our family's illness. Though this is a HPPA violation and probably worth thousands, I do not have time to pursue the offender. The laws are in place for privacy protection. Sadly, privacy is offset via social media scourges. Mandy was innocent; and felt she needed to call. I thanked her and we are having a mini-date after the frosh game early Friday evening. I am certain that Mandy and I will be a topic on social media platforms; but so be it. The New World order is no privacy (zero). I am struggling to find a quiet place for my soul; and will keep searching. My order in life is: God, family, and then teaching/coaching jobs. Girlfriends are critical, but are in 4th place until they become family – then the girlfriend relationship becomes just below God. Prayer will get me through this difficult period. I do know the rosary; and I should say portions of it daily. I am still conjuring the reason of 10 Hail Mary's with only one Our Father. I need to study the rosary. The 5 decades of the rosary require meditation from Mary (needed); and then a prayer to the real Father (not Jesus, the son). Perhaps the Our Father is such a strong prayer throughout all of Christianity. The "Our Father" prayer is beholden because it is by itself. Tradition within Catholics is phenomenal. Prayer, my life coach, and my kids will keep me strong.

I received a phone call (though my telephone number is private) from an NFL assistant who is recommending me for a pro job on the coast. He has read about both the offensive and defensive schemes that Colorado Sports Academy High School runs. He loved what I termed "carpet-bombing." The coach bragged that it was unusual with a not-so athletic team to win in Chicago and Colorado (two different football venues) a 5A state championship two years running. I thanked him and he wanted to visit. I almost said yes; but then held off confirming due to: I need to think about this. I said place everything in writing on an email; and I would get back to him. He understood my position well. He was a wonderful guy I could perceive. This just adds fuel to my mind's fire within my brain. I need to return to God, family, coaching/teaching, and place job offers down the list. Brewing on matters over days also helps; but I am a terrible decision maker until it comes to football play calling. I am quick on the next play before the last tackle has been completed. That is how my mind works. I wished my mind worked well with job offers and girlfriends.

My students took on the semester challenge of the famous writers – historically and modernly. The feedback from teaching colleagues, parents, and administration was affirmative. A couple students brought in literary names I could not recollect; but they are reading and writing – my mantra for this class. We have a great relationship; and if I coach elsewhere, I will double as a teacher if my family allows such a combination (perhaps on line). I still love in-person interactivity between students and instructors. The emotions and personal feelings are robust; and learning is enhanced as opposed to online courses. We are all students throughout our lives – framed and corrugated by our experiences, emotions, and interests. I do feel I have it decent in North Colorado Springs. Do I want to jump ship while I am prospering emotionally? It will be a tough decision to turn away big money offers. Bedtime!

Day 74

A major sports network revealed themselves today at school and administration asked me if I had time for an interview. Though it is a privacy intrusion, I want to play ball with everyone, under-react, and then determine my course. Burning bridges with attitude, avoidance, or any negative emotions is not the way to move up in our world. Fans, sports media, and frankly other coaches are interested in our offensive and defensive schemes. An advantage on the field is huge; and by the time the opposition has it conquered or adjusted, the game is over. Generally, you will not play this team again until next year with new coaches, players, and overall confusion by the next year opposition's team. There is considerable change within a school year – with players coming and going. Stability in football from Pop Warner to the professional ranks is lacking. Yearly teams require re-alignment, adding players, plays to fit the new players, new coaches, and difficult adjusting rule changes. The constant is change yearly. Pros face free agency, salary caps, cuts, and injuries. College football has evolved into pro football with players switching on a whim with money, position competition, and loss of scholarships. High school boundary requirements are a joke- because players move into other homes, lie about residency, and ask for hardship. Pop Warner is an arms race to the best players. We know who they are.

After my last English – Literature class, some prominent sports writers and media entered my office with a list of modifying adjectives on the board. The sports media staff had not witnessed these primordial English lessons for years. They loved it as we discussed how to write and what to read. I informed them that the road to success was through the English language. They all agreed and wanted to discuss the next chalk board of great writers listed – many writers respected these incredibly gifted and hard-working authors. Our culture including football was dependent upon the writers listed; and many more unlisted. I discussed how media related to the popularity of sports and football. Since the Red Barber announcing of the Brooklyn Dodgers occurred initially a century ago, we have had a slew of fabulous announcers because of the communicative and wonderful English language. My teacher Mrs. Collins slapped up on the back of the wrist if we missed a descriptive pronoun; and we would be staying after school to correctly rewrite the sentence on the backboard with 50 repetitions.

Finally, we arrived at football schemes. I revealed my playbook and showed them some X and Os on the blackboard without iPhone pictures. They were amazed and loving the varying pro and college sets on offense and defense – using standard and varied schemes. The media folks loved the "Carpet-Bombing" 2 QB attack. I explained that double bootlegs properly performed easily confused our own team and coaches. The play worked when I did not know which back had the ball. Many questions arose regarding timing, blitz preparation, and fumbles with ball handling. I stated that many great offenses in prior years (Barry

85

Switzer's Oklahoma wishbone attack) had 7 strings of offense sprinting plays the entire 100-yard football field with handoffs, pitches, passes, double reverses, and misdirects. This evolved over 2 hours with coaching and players not dropping a ball. Thus, ball security is number 1; and not handling a ball constantly can lead to a fumble. Our players handle balls walking into school. Blitzes are called by the QB with an immediate shift to the opposite side with an option run, pass, or reverse if the blitz corner, safety, or linebacker cuts deep into the backfield. If there is a clear path for 5-10 yards, our QB always takes that route. I expect zero fumbles per game. If we fumble; it is all hands-on deck to recover. We will win games statistically with no fumbles, carpet bombing QBs, and smart play. One play decides a game on offense, defense, or special teams. The media left with great articles. I was cool.

Day 75

Mandy's date after the frosh date was wonderful. Her brown eyes sparkled alongside her Jewish nose features, and long brown hair. We talked incessantly about her family, Israel, and a touch of football. I tried to center the conversation about her to reveal true interest. Smitty remarked frequently that the foibles of the girl may emanate from her and not social media. Thus, allowing Mandy to talk I will get a full expose of her character, interest in me, and her prior life. She casually discussed the annulment – which impressed myself because it revealed strength. Mandy believed in monogamy; and despite counseling the philandering continued unabated. Sadly, both families elected to end the relationship. It was as if she was never married – a nullity. I know in the Catholic religion it requires faith, money, and connections to obtain an annulment of marriage. I felt sorrow for Mandy as she expressed remorse as families wanting this marriage by parents choosing partners. There was never any love and caring apparently. These mandated partnerships may work to pass down wealth responsibly; but it is not love. Mandy is after a true partner, love and caring within the marriage. She wants children.

I asked her about what she felt about my children. She says they are lovely because she met them at the Tompkins at the original Sunday social. I mentioned that some would consider that baggage; and she replied that others would consider your kids a blessing. That was a remarkable comment. This amazing financial whiz who has been everything from head Bronco cheerleader and high school prom queen to Radcliffe sorority president and working NFL finances is wanting motherhood. Becoming a mom for many trumps life. This is serious stuff. At the end while we are eating cold food (because we discussed everything), an assistant coach from Castle Rock walked by and said hello. He was with his wife and kids. We introduced everyone; and he remarked that I was the new genius of football – not just high school. I applauded his work and said thank you. Mandy really liked and respected this coach. She casually mentioned that even within the Broncos organization the "carpet-bombing" attack is discussed. Mandy mentioned that I could monetize my creativity. I followed that religion, family, job, and then everything else was the peck order. She then asked where she stood on the depth chart. I returned that she was near the family (2nd place behind God). She liked that immensely. This girl is serious. I am amazed.

We left gracefully and decided to meet at my house on Sunday afternoon for supper with our kids. She readily agreed because we would have some time together after both Josh and Jake had early Sunday afternoon birthday parties (back-to-back). She offered to attend; but then remembered she had a ton of work this weekend and could not make the date until 4 PM. The kids will have returned to neighborhood play and the keen game – where one team guards the goal (a porch or garage), while the other hides and sneakily touches home base. This game goes on for hours until supper is called by a quorum of neighborhood moms. I am in deep over my head with this relationship. My life coach says go with what is comfortable. Apparently, I enjoy Mandy, and I am "comfortable." Goodnight!

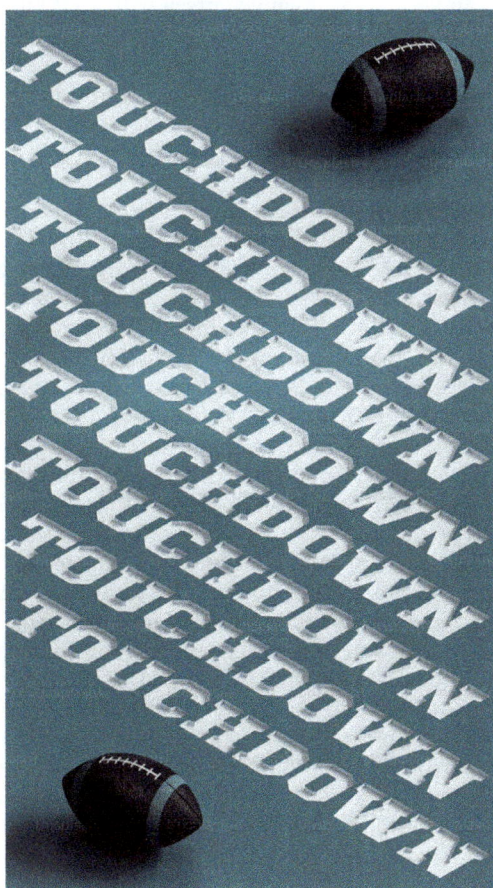

I awoke in the middle of the night because of a dream. I was sweating and drenched the bed. I was embarrassed; but recollected the dream scenario. I had met Janae at the airport and was informing her about Colorado Springs. She appeared excited. It appeared she had stayed behind in Chicago, recovered from her spreading breast cancer, and was now returning to her family and kids. We talked incessantly from DIA to our driveway; and as I opened her car door, I awoke. I asked myself what all this meant. Years ago, when Sigmund Freud evaluated dreams, they all meant something deep. I still believe that. At least the dreams reflect important matters in your life. Though surreal, during the dream it is live reality television with yourself as the actor. I discovered upon awakening that this was a dream; and Janae dying was my live nightmare. Perhaps I will never recover from grief. I surmise that we all deal with grief; and you just deal with time healing your mind and body. Occupying yourself with your family and friends is critical; that appears for me to blunt myself crying 24/7. Strong football coaches like myself have emotions and cry. I could attend counseling sessions forever; and I would still incur and maintain some periodically erupting melancholic thoughts and fun memories. The suffering Janae incurred with metastatic cancer and bone pain was beyond description. Thankfully, she is in a better place now.

I need to move on, garner more friends, and establish good relationships. Marrying would require someone extremely special; and I cannot just pretend on dates. Few our age just want to go out for fun. It is working towards a meaningful relationship that is a partnership long-term. I love the idea of establishing a new mom for these three young boys. That is an immense responsibility for a new partner; but perhaps they would love the challenge. Truly loving myself would place them beyond dealing with three kids – not considered baggage (a slang term). Everyone in a marriage has extended family, environment of work, illness, risks of kids' illness, and financial issues to confront. Marriage is not the Land of Oz. Though Janae and I loved one another, the Colorado move was a hurdle for myself to overcome after winning an Illinois 5A state high school football championship. Why would anyone run away from a highly successful now established program with recruits throughout Illinois wanting to play on your high school football team? I respected and honored Janae's wishes. That was part of the marriage pact. I was so in love that she could have requested northern Siberia and I would have capitulated. It is hard to go through this dating process again. I get it; but not crazy about having a duty to fall in love. The kids can just deal with having me be both mom and dad. Developing a relationship and partnership is nice; and I am slowly gaining ground. It is tough; because grief is tough. Possibly, Mandy is the right person. Janae's mom obviously picked her out of a litter of professional established Greenfield Village gals who are in my wheelhouse. I was down on Janae's parents for forcing this relationship stuff; but with age, perhaps they have insight and knowledge that I do not yet possess. I need to process. Time to fall asleep.

The press is on regarding myself deciding on taking another job. My mentors have all stated that many coaching jobs in established programs will always be there. Uprooting after 7 months of Colorado living is unsettling to myself. The programs keep calling and electronically contacting me with the ante rising with each phone call or email. It all appears that winning the Colorado 5A High School Championship is a big deal. Overcoming Denver clubs with established successful legacy programs was impressive. Athletic magazines, social media, and chatter makes it appear I have established a new atomic bomb in American football. The 2 QB pro-set and wishbone attack with 2 qualified QBs in the backfield has caught the sports media buzz. I do not feel there has been anything similar since the Arkansas high school football coach that never punted was the chatter. Since it is QBs, the sports whirring is louder because it is the prized critical position. Nothing has arisen in QB play since spiking the football by Dan Marino in the 1980s to stop the clock (though technically this is intentional grounding – allowed). The platoon QB, dual threat QB, and certain throws like "back shoulder" have been around for years (Marino also perfected the back-shoulder QB pass). Teams are asking a myriad of questions from QB injury risk to running plays designed for the dual threat QBs. I respond that versatility is what makes an offense dynamic. The "carpet-bombing" or "Ambush" attack is designed to confuse defenses and succumb to a simple running play up the gut for 5 yards. Defenses are so worrying about gadget plays that simple plays and blocking schemes become easier.

Smitty maintains that I need to monetize the 2 QB pro-set. I love the idea of making some extra cash; but feel I would have more stability by not having a podcast, book, or other media remuneration by just simply coaching for what I am worth on the open market. Most probably another coaching job involves a move, new friends for the kids, and leaving behind a romance. My life coach always says go with what feels right and good. There is no hurry with relationships; they just happen. I like that advice. The partner in the relationship may help guide myself on my coaching life's journey. I like that additionally. I need to prepare for tomorrow's classes with some of the book reports on famous authors. I cannot dwell on the ultimate coaching opportunity.

I tucked the kids into the Harry Potter series. They loved these books and want more. The stories are tremendous about fantasy and the wizard Harry Potter. Harry Potter is a real hero with my kids due to bravery, loyalty, and compassion. There are endless fun exciting stores. My three boys are asleep before I am done. We are a real family. And despite what has occurred, we are surviving and thriving. I do not envision my three boys ever wandering away from myself or each other. The family attachment is forever tight. I am blessed and fortunate. Good night.

Day 78

A student had a seizure in class today and required CPR. Thankfully, I have maintained my Basic Life Support every 2 years training. The cardiopulmonary resuscitation was performed by myself and students with staff assisting from nearby classrooms. It was tenuous regarding a success. My student was a female cheerleader who had worked immensely in our class and wanted to attend Stanford University. She was dazed when we finally lifted her onto the ambulance to transport her to St. Francis InterQuest in Colorado Springs. I was hopeful that there was no permanent damage. She will spend the evening; and hopefully be back in class in a couple days. I visited her at the hospital that evening after basketball practice; and many students and family were present. We discussed everything from learning English in our class to the football team and cheer squad. I spent a few minutes wishing her well; and that she could take her time finishing the week's projects. Our student had already finished today's lesson; and was working on tomorrow's lesson in fundamental English – studying sentence structure. My students and families are excited about our class; and feel this is a jump start for their careers. I walked away down the hospital hallways smiling; not crying because I have accomplished my mission of excellent instruction in English, Literature, and Composition.

Smitty arrived for some college basketball on television with a couple of beers after the hospital visit. We discussed some rule changes that were needed including: 1) Enlarging the floor with four more feet under the basket and extension laterally to allow some room for 3-pointers, 2) removing the inner circle where contact is awarded to the offense – disallowing defense to be played appropriately, 3) No replays – unable to discern who touched the ball last = a jump ball, 4) 6 fouls per player – so a player does not sit with 2 early fouls, 5) Incidental contact that does not affect the play (pass, dribble, or shooting) be a no-call. Many layups are brush or anticipatory fouls historically called which do not affect the shot. 6) No contesting the referees call in any league – live with the call, 7) 8 seconds to cross the mid-court line in all leagues, 8) one time-out the last minute to finish the game.

Smitty and I left after a couple beers thinking we could restructure the game of basketball. Generally, the better team wins; and I am quite satisfied with or without our rule changes. The kids keep calling and have not fallen asleep after a big day for the entire family. We are still reading Harry Potter and the Philosopher's Stone. I love wizardry.

Day 79

My arrival is school was met by the superintendent and principal of Colorado Sports Academy High School. The student in the hospital with the seizure has a large malignant brain tumor. I nearly cried discovering how cruel life can become. Our class was subdued today as everyone in the class, cheer squad, and school is crying or downcast. I nearly cried addressing all the students as questions were raised regarding religion, medical diagnosis, and how we can collectively assist our fellow star student and cheerleader. I replied that much of what is discussed is in God's and the medical community's hands. We can support her with visits, positives, and make her feel she is not alone in her medical fight against cancer. I mentioned that I had a prior similar bad outcome with my wife, Janae, dying from unexpected breast cancer. My situation and experience were difficult dealing with three young children and their mom advancing to heaven early. I will support her family and our student with anything she needs. This will be our class's mission – to assist where needed. We planned a Go Fund Me account, daily positive social media narratives (in proper English), and daily visits would be planned within medical constraints. She will undergo surgery, radiation, and chemotherapy over the next 2 months. Prayers daily outside of school will occur. The class was considerably more positive as we discussed the disease and our student. We all want a positive outcome.

The frosh basketball squad is advancing with our season tethering on late game free throws. I instructed the "Gather" technique to advance our percentage as the best in Colorado High School. We are missing 1-2 free throws per game. Advancements beyond this will include plain fundamentals of rebounding, passing, dribbling, execution of plays, ball screens, and immense full court pressure defense. All frosh are participating on teams, playing indoor and outdoor constant scrimmages, and parents have assisted where needed. The developmental squads are exactly what I wanted; and the school and other schools are attempting to recruit myself now as a basketball coach. I am still dealing with college and pro NFL positions; but need to decide to stay or grab a lucrative position elsewhere. I am not certain of where to go next year with so much occurring. There are windows of opportunities; and many feel I would be a fool to look the opposite way at many of these opportunities. I stare at my kids as they play with neighbor kids in our backyard and others property. I could not be happier to have them enjoy the play they have experienced. They potentially could obtain that anywhere; but I am living Janae's dream of a Colorado upbringing for our children. I am fortunate to have options and that my teaching and coaching is proceeding well. Few would not entertain a move that would provide family security forever. The kids arrived back in the house today for some late evening ice cream and Harry Potter bedtime stories. These Harry Potter book series are wonderful for kids. I will sleep tonight.

Day 80

An email arrived on my computer today at from Alison Maples DO (our former pediatrician). Alison states she is dying from end stage leukemia unresponsive to bone marrow transplants, immunotherapy, and chemotherapy. The family and Alison have elected hospice care and it is hours to days before Alison is in heaven. Alison's request included only her immediate family have contact with her. She elected to stay at the Mayo Clinic Hospice because the care was wonderful. I cried and felt how unfortunate life is for many people. Life certainly has its bumps and bruises; and is unpredictable. The entire situation is quite sorrowful regarding Dr. Maples and how she left knowing that there was something

91

seriously wrong with her body and metabolism. I feel she was embarrassed and shocked simultaneously. I could have married this woman because she was a great person and physician. The 3 kids did not bother her; and Alison would have welcomed the kids into her own sphere. Most probably Alison was infertile from her leukemia treatments of radiation, immune, and chemotherapy. She did not mention if she saved eggs before her treatment; but she probably salvaged eggs as most patients do before major surgery or intense medical treatment. Janae and I both saved our DNA. I do not know if Janae's eggs were fertilized because she died so quickly. It probably does not matter except the Catholic Church wants all these infertility clinics with frozen embryos at early cell division to be adopted. That would be a large stretch for myself; but again, things happen within families. Our kids will undergo genetic testing at The University of Colorado.

The frosh basketball team is nearing playoffs within the city. We have maintained good composure and learned immense fundamental hoops this year. Many players are playing AAU and Denver Nugget youth ball. Obviously, the parents and players want me to coach. The golf team is also asking that I coach while I muse over a myriad of offers from high school, college, and professional football. Honestly, I am not certain where to go and what to do. My life coach feels I need to go with what feels good and right. I am not certain if leaving after an undefeated season of football makes sense. Additionally, the Greenfield Village debutante, Mandy, is serious about a partnership. She is overwhelmingly beautiful and nice. The annulment does not bother me because to a football guy, an annulment is like a typical break-up at any age. The annulment is just not recorded as a divorce – like the breakups we have all experienced. I want something good to happen to make me stay in Colorado – as Janae desired. The offers I am receiving would have many coaches stating I need a new brain if I refused any of these fabulous football coaching offers.

The kids are continuing to perform well in school and preschool. I have been able to make all the birthday parties and other social events. They love having dad present. We talk about guy stuff after the birthday parties and ski outings. It is obvious the kids have adapted to Colorado much easier than I have assimilated. My acclimation is slow compared to my kids' adaptations. Thus, would my kids adapt in a new setting that guaranteed a life-long financial security scheme? Money is not everything; but it is important. I want something to happen that keeps me here. More pay would help additionally. I think about this all through the day when not teaching or coaching. The kids sense that other jobs and a possible move is in the air. I inform them before the Harry Potter read at night that presently we are staying in Colorado. Perhaps I just need to pray more for guidance.

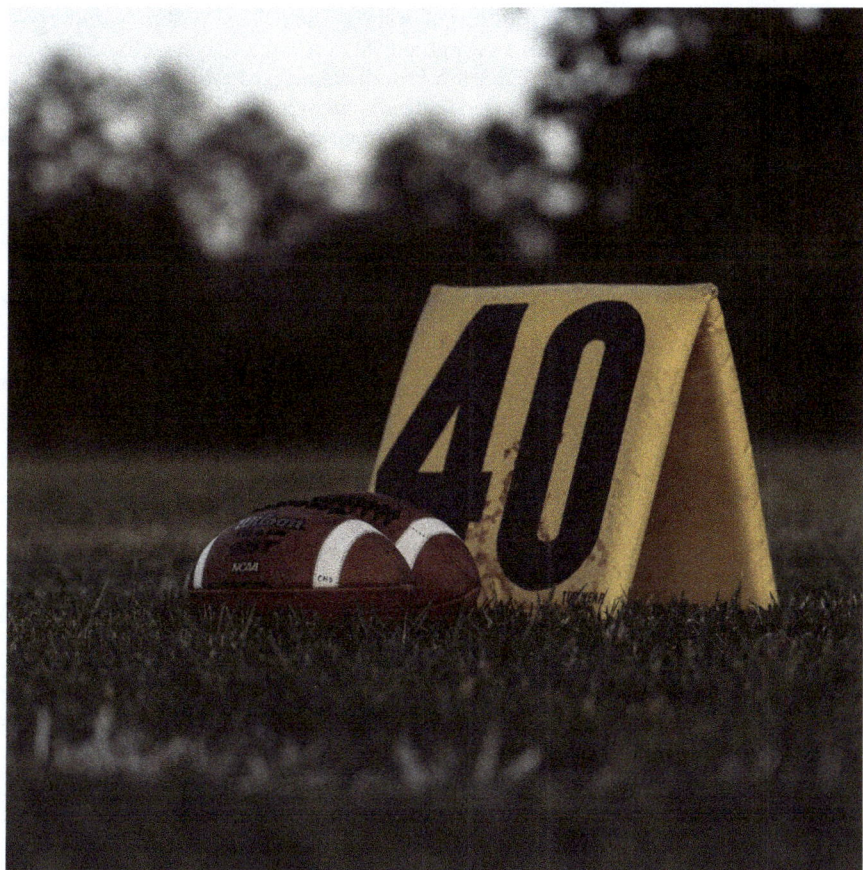

Day 81

Mandy called late last night and we talked for 45 minutes. It was delightful; and we are going to a play at the Littleton theater. We are having dinner afterwards at her house (she loves to chef). That really works because it is not far from our Monument, Colorado home (35 minutes). Mandy sounded quite interested and mentioned the Alison Maples situation – it is repeated throughout Colorado social media on many platforms. We discussed that we dated a few times, never were that serious, and her health became an issue quickly with recurrence of leukemia. Mandy felt bad for myself; but I mentioned that I am slowly adapting to life's bumps and bruises. I am moving on with relationships, planning on teaching and coaching next year, and my focus was my three boys. She was quite happy that I had my priorities correct. She discussed her job dealing with the complexities of NFL and some college level teams accounting. The NFL has salary cap issues with constraints and unfairness within the system – players on the same team competing for their share of a large amount of NFL salary cap money. Players deferring salaries is risky because a league may become bankrupt with little left for players owed millions of dollars. The college system is undergoing massive transformation with a swinging gate of money, players, contacts, and coaches. The student athlete for Division I football and basketball players is highly secondary; but everyone acknowledges this is incorrect since 3% of Division I college football players enter the NFL. The average stay rate for NFL players is 3.5 years. Collegians need their education.

Most collegiate Division I teams must win to survive. Failure to win breeds impediments to future success. The colleges at the highest level of football are professional football – watered down overall. There are massive amounts of money through media, boosters, and endowments that want to maintain winning programs at any cost. Mandy is within the sphere of accounting and advising on the limitations of NCAA money allotments and outside appropriations. She feels despite everyone down on portals and NIL (Name/Image/Likeness), there will be widespread growth of college football. The competition is ramped beyond reason; but fans are immersed because football is our sports culture modernly. Covid killed almost everything except football.

Finally, Mandy discussed the kids and wanted to do some things with our kids. Enjoying the kids was a highlight for me; because many women though interested in myself would consider the kids as "baggage." Mandy wanted to know details of my kids' friends, schools, teachers, and social adaptations to Colorado. I freely discussed their kids wanted a new mom; and probably should not have said that statement. There was quiet on the other end of the phone when I said that statement; but it could not be retracted because it was true. I jumped far too early; and it is so stupid of me. I told Mandy that I said that in jest; but she said that was probably true and kids generally spill their emotions. I am totally ahead of myself and was somewhat embarrassed; but overall, the discussion was a 10. I need to read them Harry Potter – Mandy loved Harry Potter. Perhaps Janae's mom was correct in hand-picking our kids' new mom?

Day 82

School has been fabulous for our kids Josh and Jake. Jaiden has a couple years before preschool. The nannies are loving our kids; and the neighborhood is a haven for kids playing together of all ages. Our kids fit nicely within the group and have made friends in the surrounding blocks. After homework, the kids play 4-square, the "Keen Game" from Wisconsin – like hide and seek, whiffle ball, capture the flag, soccer, tetherball, sidewalk chalk, and pickle ball on a neighbor's court. The kids argue, pick sides, perform small trash talk, and promote teamwork. I sit on our back patio and watch the joy my kids expel in good and bad weather. I generally do not bring them in until one of the surrounding moms screams for the third time to come home for supper. A neighbor down the street has an old cowbell that she rings when the evening dinner is ready. I want our kids to obtain as much out of life as we did as kids while growing up in Chicago. Many of the niceties of life are simple – such as the late afternoon early evening playtime, performing well on homework and in school, having a puppy (our Spark), and socializing at birthday and ski parties. Today as we wind down the basketball season, I am mulling over coaching opportunities that are fabulous, repeat upgraded offers (some in the millions), and long-term security for our family. I am torn between my simple happiness and peace coming inside of myself and the issue that I would be a business fool not to tackle one of these high paying college or pro football coaching jobs. It would be unusual to vault into the professional ranks; but the offer is on my plate.

Coaching a SEC school in football is a pinnacle of all coaches; and it is an email starred on my computer. I purposefully have taken my time as directed by my life coach. It is early evening and the Spring snow on our back patio is very light and beautiful. I cover the computer while my kids are 2-doors down screaming for attention and fun. I begin to drift off and in walks Mandy with a glass of Sangria wine. I am shocked because I did not invite nor expect the unexpected visit of a now acclaimed girlfriend. I am sitting on our small patio with a coaching whistle, sweats, Chicago Bulls tee-shirt, and dirty socks. My hair is a mess and I probably smell like old sweat after working with the frosh basketball team – participating in drills (which is what all coaches should do). I embrace Mandy as a welcome and she smiles with her brown hair and eyes. She appears a million dollars and smells wonderful. This is a mismatch. She brought supper for the family and a box of Sangria – pouring herself a glass. I asked where did she discover I liked Sangria? Obviously, she performed a complete background check on myself (all girls do this). Mandy said Janae and I were the talk of Chicago enjoying a glass of Sangria on Michigan Avenue after the Illinois football 5A championship win. The evening will be great!

Mandy and I had time to talk for an hour as the sun set against the Rockies. The unexpected visit and wine were tremendous and signified seriousness. I liked it. When the kids came home; Jake mentioned and asked if this was finally the new mom? I said we are working on that; and he said Dad, I need a yes or no. Mandy and I smiled and packed this into our back pocket for later discussion. After I opposed Janae's parents Sunday afternoon debutante coming out parties for weeks, I realized they may have been correct. Mandy helped with the dishes, hugged the kids, and read a story from Harry Potter's wizardry book. This is better than a football win.

Day 83

The days keep slowly lengthening as the kids played outside. We have completed a couple spring ski trips to Winter Park and Ski Granby. I now understand Janae's missing Colorado- because there is nothing close to the activities, mountain weather, and grandeur of Colorado Springs. Mandy and I had a date in a couple days after the nanny agreed to spend some extra time at our house with college homework. I probably need to have her move-in and occupy a bedroom. The kids love the nanny and backup nanny. The date with Mandy was ecstatic. We visited the Will Rogers Shrine (wonderful) and then had supper at the upper Broadmoor 1858 restaurant at the base of Seven Falls. The food was exquisite; and I mentioned it was as delightful as downtown Chicago food (some of the world's best restaurants). Mandy had never been to Seven Falls; but as a spoiled

Denverite, it was taboo to travel south to Colorado Springs. Nothing in Colorado Springs could be as nice as Denver. We laughed about such matters; and I had mentioned that when we initially moved to the front range of Colorado, the traffic was unsettling. The Larkspur Renaissance Festival was ongoing for 2 weeks; and traveling to Denver was impossible. Mandy mentioned that Larkspur was the furthest south any Denver resident would ever travel. Colorado Springs is not considered part of the discussion along the front range. The Springs is in second place.

Mandy opened about her dreams and wanting to have more children as a gulped more Sangria wine. I can have more children; and my three boys would probably love more offspring in the family. That is a monster commitment from a guy who is on overload already. It is obvious that Mandy respected Janae; and felt Janae knew how to pick husbands. Why me? Mandy stated I was a 10 in looks, alpha guy, loved sports, and had respect with my religion and teaching background. I knew she was scouring the social media platforms. I have not and will not do that with Mandy. I will take her at face value. I do not need internet support for decisions. I am thinking of my life coach Sandy stating go with what feels good. Am I falling in love?

As the sun set and the night was a touch chilly, a couple interrupted us and asked that I sign their menu for an autograph. It was obvious they were a football couple. After some small talk and some discussion about the 2 QB set, I opened my iPhone and revealed some 2 quarterback plays I have used. I informed them that variations were smothered on the internet. The couple was extremely cordial; and I would enjoy being their friends. Mandy had a nice talk with his wife. The couple then asked if we were married or getting married; and Mandy and myself stared at each other. I did not know what to say; but felt the easy answer was: "working on the relationship." They smiled and drifted away as Mandy and I smooched. We arrived home to sleepy kids who fell asleep on the couch. We placed them into beds and Mandy parted with a smile. Mandy is helping me out of my funk with resisting relationships and partnerships. It was a good night. I will not sleep; but that is fine. I could be falling in love!

Day 84

Smitty came over for some football watching and gave me a mouthful of social media about myself and Mandy. We had some discussions about relationships as his employee on and off fling is now over. The issue is that he is her superior – never a good situation. Office romances are tough – but I get how people meet. We are all capable of marrying many people. The alignment of the stars, hormone levels, compatibility, family, money, future, and entering a monogamous relationship for life matter to a high level. There are barriers in every relationship. Smitty asked how Mandy enjoyed and dealt with the kids. I replied it could not have been better; as Mandy read them to sleep, fed them, changed Jaiden's diapers, and the kids loved her immensely. Smitty felt that was a positive sign. I have a ton on my plate with semester exams, evaluating students' prose writings, and parent-teacher conferences (which I enjoy). I invite students to attend with their

96

parents so we are all on the same wavelength structurally regarding improvements academically. Few teachers employ this technique; but I find it helpful since one message is sent to the family. The parent – teacher conferences require preparation and time. Obviously Smitty pried into my job offers; and I had not seriously given much job thoughts today. I wanted to wait until the school year ended before tackling that proposal – realizing that many would be relinquished. Smitty and I discussed the issue of a partnership with Mandy and then departing for some remote job (like Baltimore) as an offensive coordinator or QB coach. I said we would cross that bridge if the relationship became more serious. We are just beginning to know one another. This will take time; but it is strongly apparent Mandy is interested in myself as a life-long partner potentially. We have a date this upcoming weekend – meeting between us in Castle Rock.

The beer and football were great. I love watching football with another footballer. We argue calls, plays, and strategy continuously. I generally think I win; as does my opponent (Smitty). Smitty feels I could outcoach most coaches presently in college and the professional ranks. I replied that was conjecture; and players, money, contracts, injuries, fans, owners, and the overall program legacy had considerable effects on the success of the program. Coaching was a part of football success; but not the entire package. Great coaching is on every winning program. Great coaches can be on lesser programs if not supported by players, management, assistant coaches, trainers, fans, and media. Alignment of many positives must occur for a winning season. I do feel I could coach college or professional football – given the opportunity. I am not certain if I should jump ship. There is a ton on my plate; and I need to finish the school year.

The phone rings and Dr. Alison Maples sister is on the phone from the Mayo Clinic Hospice. Alison has died; and she will have her body donated to the local medical school anatomy class. I was subdued, cried, and asked if there was anything I could do to help. Her sister remarked that Alison loved me, asked for your prayers, and died peacefully without pain. Her family was present; and a mini celebration of life was held at the bedside as Alison desired. Her ashes went to her sister. I said we would stay in contact because she was so nice and sincere. God Bless Alison Maples DO.

Day 85

Our family spent Sunday at the Wolf Lodge in northern Colorado Springs. We enjoyed every water ride and the lazy river. Mandy joined us as we seemed like a real family. The kids automatically feel she is the new mom. We will determine this in time. I have enjoyed Mandy's companionship. Everyone in our family loves her – as well as Janae's parents (Herb and Sherry Tompkins). Next week we are invited to a Saturday evening social at the Tompkins in Greenwood Village. The kids are also invited as neighbor kids will be attending. Mandy is highly anticipating the social since she now has an automatic date. I was wrong about the Tompkins and dissuaded myself about their Sunday afternoon socials of meeting neighbors and debutantes. I was blindly hit by an amazing woman (Mandy). I am certain many friends and family in our sphere are anticipating a proposal. I will take my life coach's advice – if it feels good, then go with it regarding relationships. I will always have grief over Janae. These are her kids. Sad, she cannot enjoy them; but we do not understand many aspects of our earthly existence. God's plan is not of our making. Life is unpredictable; and I am not surprised when jobs, relationships, or lives falter or rise. I feel that I am becoming happy again. Realistically, I need a mom for these kids; but having another 3-on-3 basketball team is somewhat overwhelming. The give and take of a relationship equate that if I marry Mandy, I must respect her wishes to have a large family along with my kids (blended). I can deal with all this having a strong partner.

The youth who had the drug issue turned his life around by attending rehabilitation, working to obtain As and Bs in his classes, and progressed in frosh basketball. I discussed the situation with his parents and they were relieved he was able to stay on the hoop team. Few people knew of his drug issue; and since this is a medical issue; federal privacy applies. I cannot discuss his situation medically with anyone excepting his family and the student. Colorado Sports Academy High School performed well because this easily could have been a suicide. I strongly wanted to avoid this by not dismissing him from his peers through sports and socialization. This could be a small bump in a future strong life because our school academically and through sports supported his academic and emotional needs.

The kids are winding up the ski season. The original ski group with Dr. Maples invited our family to an Arapahoe Basin final ski party. We have an early start, nannies and games for kids not skiing (Jake and Jaiden), and we end skiing until 4 PM with a tailgate in the parking lot. This will be ultimate Colorado; and great socialization for our kids because other young families will be present. Few places on earth have such immaculate ski resorts. Mandy is also skiing; so, we will all have a year-end ski retreat. The snow is great; and more is coming. I applied a hook with the kids – meaning we are skiing if the grades are good (not kind of). The got the message firmly. Colorado is a great place for families. I do love it here. I get what Janae meant about raising kids in Colorado. Good night!

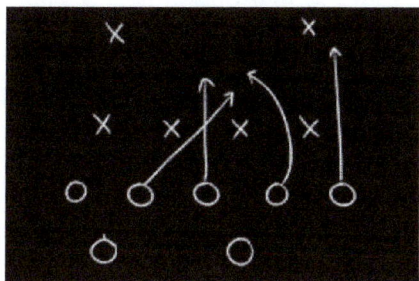

Day 86

The ski party was great according to my students who watched some of the internet videos from the kids' ski party. One of the gals asked if I was getting married to Mandy. I smiled and said we were dating. The students who revealed this to me before class instructed me that marriage would be good for me. I responded that marriage was great if it was the correct choice. An ensuing discussion began which amplified the discussion of "living together" v a celebratory marriage. Most of the gals present wanted a permanent commitment; while some of the guys wanted to test the waters with a "living in" situation. Historically, in the American culture, living together or cohabitation began in the 1960s with the sexual revolution, premarital sex, birth control pills, mini-skirts, and legal abortion as a form of birth control. Some studies relate with women first marrying under the age of 36, a 70% preemptive lengthy (years) cohabitation prior to marriage occurred. We then discussed the issues of bank accounts, kids' names, family issues, parental pressure to tie the knot, and the ability to easily leave a non-celebratory relationship without recourse. Students were involved in the discussion as I mentioned that any relationship involves commensurate reciprocal give and take. Every couple and situation are different. Generally, if only one partner wants a formal commitment and marriage, then the relationship does not continue. Ultimately, I relayed to the small group of students the importance of adult responsibility in your work, religion, jobs, relationships, and family.

As the rest of the class entered and sat, the discussion amongst my initial student group that began with an internet video of the ski party, grew to involve everyone. As a private school (Colorado Sports Academy High School), we are to a degree not limited in discussing religious related aspects. The tangential nexus if our school receiving state funding, however, has placed a vice on the school through myself or any teacher promoting or defeating any religion (widely applied). The Free Exercise Clause allows an individual to practice any religion they choose without discrimination; while the Establishment Clause disallows the government from establishing a religion – added to the Bill of Rights in 1791. Our school through receiving state funds is limited by not being able to establish a religion or promoting (establishing) the ways of religion surrounding these beliefs. This is separation of church and state; and as teachers we cannot ascribe to a certain way of life that reflects a religious belief. Students are vulnerable at young ages; and religion is firmly left to families at home and non-school practices.

99

A student then asked regarding my prayers after football games. This was an issue under Kennedy v Bremerton School District in the Supreme Court. Prayers after school are private; though on school grounds if students are not coerced into prayer or the school promoting prayer. The right for private prayer after school sports games is supported by the Free Exercise Clause and First Amendment (Free Speech). I mentioned that religion will never be part of any school receiving state funding beyond basic needs such as textbooks. Schools receiving building funds or ancillary program funding of any kind are considered public for refraining from religion adaptation within the school boundaries or school promoted events off site. I smiled as the class seemed keenly interested when I said this began with myself on a social media platform which evolved into the practice of living together (cohabitation). The discussion carried into the historical context of cohabitation after the 1960s cultural revolution of music. dress, arts, and values. Religions fostering marriage preceding cohabitation I cannot advocate or suppress because of the Establishment Clause as applied to our school. The couples, family, and religious preferences are deciding factors.

The class gained some traction on myself as having a life outside of football (girlfriend and ski party). I left with them having an electronic assignment due in a week to apply 3 synonyms and 3 antonyms to my top 100 words. There will be a written test; and a formal in class group competition – dividing the class in half – next week. The class left excited and competitive. I am hopefully being a great teacher and respected adult for my young students.

Day 87

Fearing remorse from administration, I received none after my last class discussing The Free Exercise and Establishment Clause. A couple student athletes wanted to pray after sports contests; and I said they could join without participating in the athletic contest. Word leaked within a couple days to another social media platform with the front range of Colorado and the globe focusing on our large prayer gatherings of both teams after football or basketball. The pictures and comments covered the map of opinions; but generally, were positive. Many coaches and teams that want me to coach at their programs next year applauded the move. I replied via a simple thanks. Many kids have no recourse when their parents are non-religious (agnostics) or atheists. I feel sorry for these kids and families; but everyone in life deals with uphill struggles and impediments. It seems I am a celebrity without wanting to be a celebrity. People that want the celebrity statues are welcome to my privacy invasion. I cannot go to church or walk off a sports field without some social media magnification or recourse beyond my control. Perhaps in time (when and if we lose), the magic and excitement regarding myself and the football program will evade social media popularity.

Smitty arrived over for some Thursday Night Football after the kids were down. We discussed the offense with an Xs and Os clipboard. Smitty wanted to add a couple wrinkles to the 2 QB offense with a double bootleg RPO (run – pass option). This was interesting; but was timing and blocking dependent. One QB received a snap at center, faked a power run, and then bootlegged to the strong side. If there was a pass, run crease, or offensive advantage, the QB ran or passed. If the play was stuffed, a reverse handoff occurred to the flanker (our 2nd QB). The 2nd QB had the same options as the QB #1 headed up field on a post pattern. The fake handoff, bootleg, and handoff must be practiced consistently daily to perfect the sequence. This differed from a jet sweep because of the fake power run initially, the bootleg, and the 2nd back (our 2nd QB) having a RPO with the designated receiver QB #1. All other skill players (tight end, receivers, and running back) will block. The power runner receiving the fake handoff aims for the middle linebacker. The lone receiver is QB #1 because the play is designed to massively confuse the defense and allow a run-pass option by both QBs. I mentioned that the play required great blocking and timing. The ball is thrown away by QB #2 if there is no open receiver (QB #1) and no open daylight. I told Smitty we would discuss it with the assistant coaches. The beer tasted great after a long day.

Mandy called and wanted to know what was happening in Colorado Springs with the notoriety about us as a couple, prayers after football games, and parents all over the state wanting into my English, Literature, and Composition Class. She mentioned that I taught cursive writing, fundamental English, and studied the great writers globally. Mandy wanted to attend the class. I humored her by stating there was a waiting list; and I would give her my last assignment of 100 words needing synonyms and antonyms. She mentioned that she was discovering good things about me daily. Mandy loved it because she received some positive calls and emails from many of her friends. Many told her to not let this guy go. I laughed as we planned tomorrow night on our back patio watching the kids play in the back neighborhoods, the hide and go seek "Keen" game from Wisconsin.

Day 88

The athletic director called about assistant coaching the men's golf team for the rest of the year. A coach left over a contractual issue; and the team needs assistance. I mentioned that my handicap was 3; and the AD was ecstatic. I have coached golf prior; and love the game. I said I would help as a consultant and could not be there nightly. We are finishing our frosh basketball tourneys – which has required a ton of time. I discussed some innovative ways to manage sports which drew a sigh from the AD. Beginning at 0600, teams could practice at various times during the day by extending the school day. The extra time would include intramurals, extracurricular activities such as speech and debate, and clubs. Students would become adjusted to a college schedule. We already have late buses; so that issue would be solved. A student's academics schedule could rotate around his gym and extracurricular activities. A student could have an 0700 academic start, basketball at 1100 hours, and perhaps musical practice at 1500 hours. The gyms and practice fields would be used constantly. Personally, I would not mind having a 0630-football practice and be done at 0800 hours. Students and faculty could choose their optional classes surrounding the schedule. A specific history class may be elected as a junior instead of sophomore year. I also mentioned that year-round school with a month off in the summer would be advantageous for many students. Fulfilling college requirements in 3 years

101

to move on makes more sense than a scattered summer. School and fall sports practice begin early and are year-round with 7x7 football all summer. Most of our students will advance onto college and graduate school – this would cut the years down. The AD was intrigued.

Josh has another birthday party near Castle Rock this weekend. It was too late to order from Amazon; so, I visited a nearby Walmart in Castle Rock – a few miles north off I-25. While browsing and choosing some Harry Potter books, a Denver coach fist-pumped me. We talked football for nearly 45 minutes while my kids ran the isles and played. His older daughters were whining until they got on their IPhones and social media platforms. We discussed some plays, recruiting, and next year's schedule. He mentioned his team was probably adopting the 2 QB backfield set. He applauded myself for changing football for the better with more offensive innovation. I thanked him; and we elected to perhaps socialize at the upcoming summer Colorado Coach's Conference. He mentioned to me that I was undoubtedly receiving Colorado High School Coach of the Year. I was humbled; and did not realize such an honor existed. We then delved into the college and professional offers. His experience was similar – finishing runner-up 3 years prior and being offered many upgraded jobs with small kids. His family came first; and he loved where he was residing in Denver. That was a good decision for him; but not everybody. His wife was involved in the church and had many great friends. He could not at that time just move to Florida or Arizona. We parted with contact information exchange.

I purchased a couple more Harry Potter books for our kids (Chamber of Secrets and Prisoner of Azkaban). The kids want to go to bed early so we can read as much as possible. I mentioned it was a deal. They were quite happy; and I realized all kids need is parental love for success. Everyone deserves this in life; though many do not receive love. We drove into our driveway and the kids asked if Mandy could read the books tonight. They also remarked that Mandy was probably our new mom? Kids reflect life!

Day 89

The day crept on myself until I realized I was needing to get to this birthday party near Castle Rock. I wrapped the Harry Potter books and wrote a card from Josh – not bad for a guy coach. We all jumped into our SUV and there was a road block on I25 immediately. The police were rerouting traffic to a county road. Now, I am considerably late. My son Josh was not happy – thinking the party would be over and the birthday song sung by our arrival. We did arrive an hour late while just beginning the birthday song. We joined in as Josh stared at myself. I will never forget that stare; nor will I ever be late again for a birthday party. Josh joined in with the presentation of the first gift which the birthday girl and family loved (Harry Potter books). Thus, I gained a few points from the birthday crowd and my son. The games began after the cake and ice cream and birthday gifts were opened. It was a fun occasion for the kids. I apologized to the mom of the girl and noticed that she was single. I also noticed that she was excessively smiling and asking a ton of questions about football and my career. The other parents were moms. I was embarrassed at being hustled again. I tried to be nice and always told myself (like my QBs) to underreact to a bad call. This is a mere bad call – I think.

The mom was gorgeous, single, and the dad was a physician who I now know married the office nurse after she was dumped. This is apparently a common scenario – since the doc spends more time with his RN than his family. Obviously, the birthday gal's mom is receiving the Colorado 10-year 50% alimony barring remarrying. The new alimony recipient generally lives with the new partner the full 10 years because Colorado law requires a ceremonial marriage for the alimony to end (I have been told all these facts by the birthday mom host; and it has been court tested). The birthday girl's mom would not let go of myself. I understand with kids she is on limited time to date. I am within her wheelhouse and prey. There must be many forlorn single gals in Colorado – because I have met most of them in a short period of time. Though this would be a big blend, I feel sorry for the birthday mom. My relationship with Janae had none of these decrepit elements of non-love after marriage – which she is experiencing. It is obvious many people just cannot get along.

The birthday party ended with the birthday mom giving me a big squeeze on the arm while parting. The kids came home and played in the neighborhood after one hour of homework and reading were accomplished. Smitty came over for some early night football and we talked the birthday situation. Smitty felt I was a hot commodity on the market – good looking (how can a guy discern looks?), great coach, nice kids, and good job. This is what young adult women want – they are not looking for transient rock stars, business money gobblers, struggling mental health males, or men with fantasies never going anywhere. Young adult women will accept some baggage except the guy himself cannot be a failure to thrive. The phone rings amidst this conversation and a great football game. It is the birthday gal's mom inviting me to a social party next week down the block – a block party. I declined because (though she was gorgeous and needy), I have enough on my plate. I did not want to screw up matters with Mandy. Smitty laughed and said he could only find a miserable office romance not going anywhere but south. I mentioned that we both could use wives; but if life demanded we assume both parental roles forever (as now), then that is our fate.

The kids came in for supper and we began reading Harry Potter and the Chamber of Secrets. They could not obtain enough interest. All three loved the book – though Jaiden could hardly understand. The pictures were great and the late birthday party arrival was now forgotten. I did well as a widower picking a girl's birthday present. I am moving on.

Day 90

I am concerned that all this social media chatter (which I cannot maintain interest) is upon myself. I can handle the non-personal stuff – giving credit to my assistant coaches and players who practiced my 2 QB schemes. The new offensive schemes won a Colorado 5A Football Championship my first year; and it was a back-to-back with the 5A Illinois High School Football Championship the year before. Wilford Tremby's Carpet Bombing Offense is now being termed the Rocky Mountain Arsenal with not one, but 2 dual threat QBs in the backfield. I still enjoy calling our offense simply: "The Ambush." This is altering life in the United States because football is enmeshed into our culture. I have designed plays that would confuse God according to the sports media. It has become the number one sports topic on the internet. I am deluged with mail, email, texts, and offers to coach from Pop Warner to the professional ranks. The defensive genius sports reporters on all the major sports networks are befuddled by the trickery, boot legs, RPO (run-pass options), misdirects, and mass confusion amongst the primary, secondary, and third level of defense (line, linebackers and corners and safeties respectively).

The high school students come to our English, Literature, and Composition Class revealing on their Iphone more plays discussing the Xs and Os of our offense. The championship game dual QB option that resulted in a 45-yard gain to the house was in a myriad of platforms. I enjoyed watching the play develop more than the QB trickery. The blocking schemes with the tight end and wideout destroying the outside linebacker and defensive end when it appeared the run was in the opposite direction (misdirect) was intriguing. The world can show that clip a thousand times. I am wanted on the sports media platforms live or on Google, Facebook, Instagram, You-Tube, and Twitch. I am being offered substantial amounts of cash to explain my football offense. Many teams are adopting variations of the offense. I humbly have been called Bill Walsh II. The offense is beyond the spread, power spread, air raid, or high-speed attack offenses. The Rocky Mountain Arsenal or Tremby Carpet-Bombing Attack can also perform power running. The mass confusion on defense with 2 QB options is the ultimate danger to the opposition.

Limited comments from myself to Missy Bradford from the Denver newspapers have highlighted my feelings about great athletic/Hall of Fame caliber QBs sitting on the bench or sending in complex or fake signals. These great QB running back athletes can sit for years with a clipboard and develop body and mind atrophy. I would rather these athletes play flag in the parking lot while the game is ongoing. Subbing QBs (the old way) after a blowout is not my idea of best use of athletes. I answer questions about injuries; and possibly one or both QBs going down. I reply that a virus, sprain, head injury, or fracture can happen at home or on the field – life has risks. My teams have 5 players that can play QB; and all practice the 2 QB backfield schemes. Some of these great athletes are also wideouts, corners, and punt returners. Good athletes have been throwing footballs for years; and I cringe when Sunday afternoon announcers direct intelligent football offenses to a chalkboard QB sitting awaiting his time (really?). Who started this 2nd string QB chalkboard sideline stuff? I can understand waiting your turn as an astronaut for the Space Shuttle (only a couple spots). There are gobs of high school, college (many divisions – D1, D2, D3, NAIA, Ca college leagues, club sports), and professional teams (32). All of them have backfield thoroughbreds with sideline chalkboards and cameras upon them. These benched QB athletes are thinking of U-Haul trailer hitches onto their dated vehicle after the season.

Finally, I read that QB stats from The Rocky Mountain Arsenal because of 2 or more backfield QBs would not engender college scholarships, All-American, or Pro Bowl awards. Quarterback statistics would be watered down. I say phooey! Winning is the goal; and if I cannot win with lesser athletes, then I am not a good coach. It is like a coach playing chess without your Queen. The coach deals with the no Queen on the board; and still wins. It was quite a day – goodnight. The good athletes will shine under my Ambush Offensive Football Attack. I am humbly - football.

Day 91

Mandy calls the next day while I am giving the nanny instruction for Jaiden's day. Josh goes to school by walking a couple blocks with me; while Jake heads to day-care with me a half-mile away. Mandy and her family have been reading all this social media content. She asks when will I decide about next year. I mention that my contract is up this summer for Colorado Sports Academy High School. I have not committed many crimes so I will probably be renewed. Mandy mentioned this media attention was beyond the Nuggets, Broncos, Rockies, and CU teams. Your little high school team has garnered the interest of the globe. Non-football fans are now becoming fans – wanting to see this 2 QB backfield set. Your football genius is akin to winning the lottery. And it is not going away – like politics. The football chatter is fun, entertaining, and is our culture. When I consult for college and pro sports teams accounting, there is background talk of Tremby's Carpet-Bombing Attack. Since I am in Colorado, they ask me if I know this football coach. I generally hesitate and say I have met him. If I say we are dating; then the world IT chatter will engulf me – perhaps more than you. I have accounting jobs to finish with changing sports platforms such as portals, NIL deals, college money from media (billions), and NFL salary caps. I am deluged with NFL requests for calculating deferred contract costs with depreciation, annuities, and inflation. I need to keep my mind on my job until I receive a bevy of phone calls from friends and families who say: "Did you see the latest Coach Wilford Tremby social media chatter?"

Mandy says I am now a verified "Rock Star." I laugh and she asks where do we go from here? Mandy has concerns that the divorced gal in Castle Rock at the site of Josh's birthday party is an issue. The IT chatter says we were now a "thing." I explained what happened (nothing). I mentioned I have confronted every forlorn single gal in Colorado hunting for a mate. I mentioned with teaching, now a golf assistant coach, and English/Literature/Composition High School Instructor, I am overburdened with 3 small boys – my primary focus in life. I am the mom and dad. Mandy mentions that I probably can travel nowhere and not be unnoticed. I said that will fade with time. I am overwhelmingly more concerned with my family than anything else in life. I am following Janae's directives to raise the kids in Colorado, find a mom, and live your life (which was stolen from her).

Mandy begins to cry and remembers how good Janae was as a friend living down the street. I mentioned that I fought myself over attending the Tompkins Sunday afternoon socials in Greenfield Village. I am now happy that I overcame my reservations and listened to Herb and Sherry Tompkins. I think they "get" my situation as much as myself. I could have stayed in Chicago, kept winning with my inner-city football team, and never have seen yourself or the Rocky Mountains. What a loss! I am fortunate that our family is finding our way. I am not wealthy financially; but am super wealthy from a family perspective. I will see you tomorrow night on our back patio if it does not rain – watching the kids play. I will make supper; and have a bottle of wine. Mandy says it is a deal!

I had a wonderful evening with Mandy. We both laughed because a previous divorced gal also named Mandy at a birthday party for Josh, attempted to get cozy with myself. I mentioned that Colorado has run out of guys; and Mandy stated "real guys." I find that hard to believe with rodeo, fly-fishing, football, Olympic Training Center in Colorado Springs, and skiers everywhere. Mandy states these real guys are swooped quickly. Mandy admitted she is quite picky with dates and relationships. Her first entrance into permanency failed with an annulment ending. That was difficult; but necessary. She has reclaimed her sanity, goals, and moved out of a short clinical depression after the breakup. Mandy felt like a failure; and her family doctor recommended Saffron. The Saffron helped immensely with sleep, mood, and all bodily functions. She still uses it in lesser amounts off Amazon. I am impressed that Mandy was so honest with myself. Initially, all the social media hype about my football coaching was intimidating. She informed her family and friends that at heart I am a high school teacher of English, Literature, and Composition. She informed her friends that I am over-coming a ton by losing Janae (whom she knew and respected). We met by chance at the Tompkins house; and the rest is history. I have not and will not perform social media research on her; because I like Mandy at face value. If she robbed 50 banks; it would not affect myself because she has been wonderful to myself and family. Mandy and I parted the evening with love and smiles. Things are good between us.

The kids enjoyed Mandy reading them to sleep with Harry Potter. Jaiden under-stood a small amount; but loved the pictures. The kids want her as their mom; and I said we are working on that aspect. Josh asked why I am waiting. I in-formed him that courtship requires some time; and I want it to be perfect if she does come into our family. We also discussed that more brothers and possibly sisters would come into our family. Josh was quite in agreement that having more kids in the family was a blessing. He loves his brothers (Jake and Jaiden). We are entering a new phase of life for our family; and we all want to do it right.

The discussion with Josh at bedtime turned into his fright over possibly moving again. He knows I am a good coach with many great offers; but he loves being near his grandparents. He has a plethora of friends at school and within the neighborhood. The discussion was moving and very informative for myself. It would be difficult to move away and abandon our great situation we have found in North Colorado Springs. I left the bedroom nearly crying. I have it good here; and moving away for more money and coaching prestige is risking a worse situ-ation for my kids. I also must balance my happiness here with financial security that lofty coaching jobs would bring to our family. At present on balance, I am not leaving Colorado Sports Academy High School. I must do the dishes before my bedtime.

Day 93

Smitty came over the next night for some football after the kids were tucked in. His kids have a buzzer wherever they are to alert Smitty if he is needed. The buzzer is in their pockets; and it has never sounded. His kids are older than mine; and I cannot leave my children at this young age. We discussed his girlfriend situation with an employee. Smitty is the superior; and it becomes dicey with employment evaluations, expectations, following orders, and job performance. A lover generally gets a pass until the rest of the employees complain. Smitty realizes it is not the best situation; but it is working. He does not feel it will result in a permanent relationship; but things may grow and prosper. Smitty feels I am fortunate to have met some nice girls who are looking for a gem of a guy. Smitty admits the social media chatter is overwhelming – because it is beyond all the Denver sports teams, Olympics in The Springs, and the usual Colorado stuff about skiing, mountains, and bicycling trails. Colorado is just different with some intriguing sports. Smitty rides the Sante Fe Trail weekly; and travels to Cheyenne Canyon for some skilled mountain bike trail riding. I may join him in the off-season. Colorado mountain biking like skiing is new to myself.

I arrive in class the following day and I am met by a family with a student struggling in my class. We discussed the intensity and breadth of English, Literature, and Composition. The girl was crying and did not feel she could finish the semester. She has been ill with nausea and vomiting; and has had to leave class frequently. The leaving is somewhat disruptive; but tolerable. I know she can perform the work; and I offered her to complete the course in the summer. She had finished much of the classwork until the past couple weeks. The gal was a junior and wanted to attend teachers' college. While we were discussing options, the mom quietly asked when her last menses occurred. She sobbingly stated she missed her last period. The stare from her parents arrived within 5 milliseconds. I stated that I would work with her if she was pregnant. The situation was overwhelming; and I felt quite sorry. Hopefully our student and family will be able to find peace. The home situation may be difficult. Keeping the baby is not my responsibility regarding counseling; and professional help is present. I have my own religious convictions; but I cannot transpose my feelings onto another who is probably in a precarious position. Years ago, pregnant high school women left the state and were boarded at far away homes for pregnant girls, foster homes, and high-risk antenatal units. The practice of moving away if pregnant has thankfully ended. I also envision her life at home with these parents as uphill. I will pray for this pregnant girl student and family. It is time for bed.

Day 94

Yesterday was a wonderful day. The pressure continues to mount for myself regarding replying to many football coaching offers. I am in a quandary regarding many of these fabulous jobs. I want to secure my family financially; yet the opportunity at present is not in Colorado. A move is highly doable, but not easy. Our kids would not be happy for a period – especially Josh. I was raised in inner city Chicago and never left. It was my world. I realize the world has changed by

more mobility. I have job offers in the Chicago area and in almost every state. The money for many of the coaching gigs is guaranteed. Football is supreme; and a way of winning with a de novo coach, player, offensive or defensive scheme would appear better in a football program's resume. One extra win in an SEC school would maintain the entire athletic department's numerous jobs. There is no end with American football – as it continues to escalate in popularity yearly. Improved training, techniques, players, coaches, knowledgeable fans, dream stadiums and practice facilities, media coverage 24/7, and money from all sources have made our gladiator game supreme. Years ago, American Football overtook baseball as the national pastime. I am the benefactor of such excitement and fanaticism. Then again, I have a family, solid girlfriend, stability, Colorado (Janae's wish), nearby grandparents, and skiing (which I am beginning to enjoy). Life here in North Colorado Springs is wholesome.

The English, Literature, and Composition Class has circled around to American authors and their writings. Politically a school, student, administrator, or parent could find a squabble with any writer – be it political philosophy, sexual innuendoes, 4 – letter wordings, non-discussed topics at the dinner table, and anything non-Disney or flowery. Thus, boldly I stated we will study Phillip Roth, the prolific American writer who has published 30 novels – eight have become movies. I gave the class a week to order and read "Goodbye-Columbus." Contained within the book report are the book's title and author, plot summary, character summarizations, themes, writing style, and personal reaction to the book. Roth as an atheist contradicted the strict middle class Jewish upbringing; and questioned many facets of American life and relationships. Roth's writing awards are immense – including the National Humanities Medal granted by Barrack Obama in 2011. A street in his hometown, Newark, New Jersey, is named in his honor. My students' eyes and brains will be opened by Roth's fiction and semi-autobiographical writing nature – always reviewing the past's customs and history. Roth was a brilliant complicated author who stretched the literature world with works such as "Indignation." I could become a hero high school instructor; or become a battered washed-up teacher by bringing Roth into our class. We need to get away from Shakespeare for some time.

Mandy called and wanted to talk about her troubles with the massive accounting expenditures of Ticketmaster, club seats, stadium retention or PSL (Personal Seat License), parking, food, rental space surrounding stadiums, and streaming costs. The massive expense of college and professional sports has boomeranged back to professional owners and colleges expecting a return on their investments. The athletic expenses have paralleled the revenue stream – including massive player and coach salaries, medical teams, stadium rentals, security, food outsourcing, equipment, locker rooms, training facilities, travel, insurance, and injury costs. The balance of the expenses requires her accounting to provide a framework for advertising and media costs (paying for most capitalistic United States sports teams). I listen and then say, why cannot we continue the discussion tomorrow night on our back patio with a barbecue. She agrees!

Day 95

Today was met by some student angst over Phillip Roth as our chosen author. Due to his popularity, I wanted the class to experience some real college literature. I was commanded to read Goodbye Colombus as a college freshman. I was entrenched and read many of Phillip Roth novels. In time, we will study many other authors and writers. Roth also wrote for magazine and other publications. Roth is a strong part of the American literature culture. Roth transcends common threads of racism, religion, conventionality of many cultural aspects of our society, and better than anyone looks back and questions his selfhood amongst his community. I want our students enraptured to read Goodbye Columbus in one or two settings; and crank a self-made book report without AI.
Smitty came over during the Mandy backyard date. Mandy and Smitty enjoyed one another immensely. Both felt I was treading on thin ice by using Roth as a

featured American author. I felt it was like our 2 QB offensive attack. When we started the new Carpet Bombing or Rocky Mountain Arsenal Offense, the players and assistant coaches were in disbelief. I want the simple "Ambush" offensive scheme to resonate. Our offensive and ball handling skills improved immensely. The team enjoyed being innovative and different. Many players were involved instead of the rote famous QB situation; and then there is everyone else. A QB on Tremby's team will not obtain the best QB stats; but has wins beyond the competition.

Smitty was gaining advice from Mandy regarding the office romance that has its ups and downs. Mandy instructed him to either develop the relationship or venture back to strictly employer/employee status. Most relationships as adults need to advance and not tread water. This was an enlightening discussion by my girlfriend and neighbor. I loved it. The food was perfect; and the kids played until the backyard barbecue table was set. It was a fast supper for the kids; and back to playing in the backyard before bedtime. The homework had been completed. After darkness set in, baths, and then Harry Potter read by Mandy. The kids highly enjoyed her reading the wizardry writings (genius).
Mandy had an early streaming meeting as we parted. She then asked me where the relationship was going? I somewhat expected this question since we are compatible. I answered that I was serious, we kissed, and then decided for a Denver rendezvous this weekend with grandparents babysitting. I feel very good and warm regarding Mandy. If we marry, I have already had the eye test with our kids. She loves them; and I love the relationship. Everything fits. I need some sleep.

We all struggle in life at times. Perhaps struggling is equal and we all deal with varying situations differently. Life stressors place us close to the functional line. If one drifts below the functional line because of stress, aberrant behavior, job losses or failure occurs, and relationships become negatively impacted with accelerating financial woes. Thankfully, I have overcome much of the expected grief and have dealt with Janae's passing reasonably well. Mandy discussed that situation with myself; and wanted to know if I was ready for a permanent relationship. Extended severe grief with behavioral aberrancies such as depression are common. I have my low moments while dropping kids off at functions, observing other moms with their kids, and sleeping alone. Football and sports along with the kids' school and activities has maintained my conscious. Subconsciously, I know I am still suffering to a degree. The life coach has helped immensely; and she feels it would be good for myself to have a long term opposite sex partner and eventually marry. The situation must be nearly perfect. I do believe I have that in my life now. I do not want to endlessly date. Somehow, women in young adulthood looking for a partner seem to feel I have looks and I am a good catch (social media stuff). Colleagues, friends, peers, and neighbors anticipate that I am going somewhere up the ladder within sports. I honestly do not know what to do about many of these offers; and they keep entering my mailbox and computer.

My biggest concerns are my kids (Janae and my prizes). The kids are incredibly strong through losing their mother. They have been fabulous with myself; and appear to get that we are all grieving together. Yet, we all have one another. We will see Janae in our next life. My 100% goal is to provide love and parenting to my three boys. The boys mean everything to myself. I told Mandy that occasionally I have mini-flashbacks; and could almost cry over the events of Janae's metastatic cancer diagnosis and eventual brutal clinical course. Mandy understands this quite well; and does not feel this is a weakness. Mandy asked me about my background check on her. I informed her that I do not intrude into privacy. Mandy admitted that as a Williams College student she was involved in a stunt by helping to dig a large B into their rival Amherst's football field. The Williams Dean of Students discovered who the culprits were and disciplined them by requiring us to repair the field in front of Amherst faculty and students. This is still on the social media platforms – though buried deeply. I replied that I wish that was the least of my pranks. Mandy replied that she already knew about the panty raids (a thing of the past) that I participated in at Northwestern in Chicago. That was embarrassing to get caught! Goodnight.

Day 97

Our English, Literature, and Composition High School class has resoundingly responded to the Phillip Roth assignment by reading Goodbye Columbus and then mastering a non-AI book report. The short story was published in 1959; and engendered massive discussion amongst the students about the book's topics, writing in the 1950s, and Roth himself. I loved the in-depth class discussions and book report writings. I reiterate that writing is not a lost art. One can generate prose and writings of all kinds from IT engineering; however, it is not yourself writing the piece. There is no satisfaction in copying a piece that the internet produced. Most students agreed; and many scholars within the class wanted to read more Roth this summer. I believe I achieved some literary enlightenment from our class. Only one student brought up her mom as detesting the works of Roth; but the student was allowed by her parents to read Goodbye Columbus. I received no rebuttal from teacher colleagues or administrators. I feel I have progressed our class by the end of the semester into markedly enhanced appreciation of English and Literature. The book reports were required cursive; and the writing legibility is steadily improving. I could not be happier for my class. I am in my academic element.

Smitty arrived over late for a beer after the kids were tucked in with an alarm should help be needed. We shared a couple beers and Smitty was so happy about Mandy. Smitty asked several poignant relationship questions; and I replied the relationship was evolving. Both of us were enjoying one another. The partnership with Mandy and myself was transforming positively; and we have become closer weekly. Smitty wished he had such a situation with his on and off again relationship with a coworker. Smitty also mentioned that this was the second time around for both parties; and both of us have major commitment concerns. I replied that life was tough; and if it was not right for one party, then it is not right for both parties. The relationship or partnership must ascend and be fruitful. If not, it is time to move on.

The talk between us two guys ended in football discussions about my alternating blitz packages – keeping offenses confused about blocking responsibilities. The day of lining up and facing your opponent with blocking and tackling schemes is gone. Trickery, fakes, blitzes, changing from man to zone defense pre-snap causes mass confusion on offensive blocking, pass routes, and QB timing. I pride myself equally on the defensive coaching side of the ball. Smitty wants me to stay in the neighborhood forever because of our small guy talks and kid friendships. Smitty is probably right!

Day 98

Today was enlightening in the classroom and now helping with the golf team. I discussed fundamental swing dynamics; and said swings deviating substantially from Ben Hogan's 5 Lessons of golf were doomed to failure. Ever student received a copy of the book and is required to read and study the book over the next week. I will be in golf camp with the team 2-3 training sessions per week. I love the game and teaching youth. I will play some holes and an occasional round with the golf team at Colorado Sports Academy High School. I prefer the practice tee and chipping and putting greens with learners. There is fabulous potential in many of these youth golfers. I was adamant regarding non-cutting of kids for all of youth sports. I want our kids playing; and our kids will perform fundraisers for balls, clubs, and green fees. I do feel our team needs not everything handed to them. I want parents involved on the golf team and through fundraisers. We will procure money from many sources because golf is an expensive sport. The coaches are on board with many of my ideas. I instructed the kids that it is yourself v the golf course. It matters not what your opponent scores. We need as a team and individuals to conquer the golf course. Our home course is the nearby USAFA. We have already completed a deal to keep youth golfers playing nearly daily. The course is extremely picturesque against the Rocky Mountains. I only saw skyscrapers on Chicago golf courses – incredibly crowded.

The kids enjoyed 45 minutes of Harry Potter before bedtime. The wizardry becomes intense with each page of the book. Jaiden appears to understand myself. This is an advance over the pictures within the book. Jaiden does not fall asleep until his brothers have crashed. Eventually, they all fall asleep while I am reading. I have the three of them in one room presently; but plan on separate rooms when the fighting begins (soon). My kids seem happy. The oldest Josh is pushing me into a proposal for Mandy. I said I am considering it. We talked about the responsibilities of a new mom entering the house and becoming like Janae. Josh stated I would have it easy if Mandy helped with dishes, wash, house cleaning, and nanny pickups. We will get to that point in time; but I am trending with courtship presently. Josh asks how long is courtship? We finally resolved to inform Josh immediately when and if I proposed marriage to Mandy. Josh wanted to know ahead of time. We discussed potentially having more children; and he was quite excited about more siblings. I remarked to him that Mandy wanted 3-5 children. That would make the Tremby family large – a baseball team.

The final discussion with my youthful first grade son was possibly moving. He was quite rigid in not wanting to move because he just moved from Chicago. Josh has many friends and loves the neighborhood. We both concluded that we loved our plight in North Colorado Springs. Life is leaning positively for our family. We have worked hard for proper schools, involvement, and my job and coaching roles. We would dislike our family to be miserable despite having more money. These are strong family issues to contemplate over time. I love that my kids are healthy and we have great life options. We will sleep well tonight.

Day 99

Summer is just around the corner. I am planning flag football for the team with 7on7 practices. We have many teams throughout the state that want to play Colorado Sports Academy High School. The opportunities to improve in all areas through the summer are plenty. We have many kids transferring into our school from New Mexico to Wyoming. There is a myriad of issues with regionality, tuition, home address, grades, and living situations. The athleticism of many footballers is immense. The youth football team wants to improve, win, and learn more fundamentals. Our high school is quite fortunate in now having a stellar reputation. My top 2 assistant coaches are gone through head coach recruitment from excellent programs. I was extremely excited for the coaches and families. They were highly deserving.

I woke up early today with a light alarm. A well-paid football podcast wanted me as their featured coach. It was tremendous fun discussing football history and many of our offensive and defensive plays. I reiterated my stance of having my best players on the field during competitive football in all leagues. The 2 QB backfield set generated immense chatter from the listeners and lead podcaster. The talk discussed injuries, fatigue, experience, and innovation. I flatly held that many football theories are false. Quarterbacks with ability holding clipboards, running similar plays that were developed 100 years ago, and inability to take advantage of offensive or defensive weaknesses and confusion were my sticking points. One caller mentioned that if 2 QBs became injured, a near forfeit would be inevitable. I responded that we have 3 other QBs who also play flanker, wideout, running back, and corner. The lower string QBs are repping as much as the first string; and play backfield in game situations. The podcast was extremely entertaining for myself. We will perform another football podcast shortly.

115

Mandy called in an anxious mood. She was confronted by her parents, friends, and family about our relationship. They all seemingly love me after we have met and interacted. She was blunt and stated that many in her sphere of influence state because of my widower status and social media chatter, that I would linger in our relationship. Mandy was concerned about the permanence of the relationship, where it is going, love, and what next? I was spellbound, stunned, and speechless. Every guy envisions these moments in time are coming. Succinctly, I reiterated love by stating that I had very strong feelings of affection, care, and attachment. I did not want to date forever; and I was intending to bring some matters to our attention soon. Mandy was relieved, stated she loved the kids, and long term wanted to embark on having children herself. We had not arrived at this juncture yet in the relationship; and many things can be overcome (Catholicism v Judaism). Mixed religious marriages are perhaps a cultural roadblock to marriage a couple of generations prior. I mentioned that our relationship transcended religion, social media platform jabbering, occupation, and outside influences. Mandy mentioned that if the offered coaching opportunities were where I wanted to be, then she was accepting. I may not sleep this evening. We hung up with an: "I love you."

Day 100

The day was highlighted by myself with a "wake-up' call about my relationship with Mandy. I could not keep my mind off many aspects of our phone call last evening. I am now months from Janae's death – nearly a year. Janae wanted me to move on, marry, obtain a great woman as a mom for the kids. We will see each other in our next life. I will grieve forever; but must move on for the sake of my children and myself. There is no perfect scenario about engagement. After not sleeping last evening, I realized I could lose Mandy. Women tire waiting for marriage proposals; and it is not fair that it is under my control. Mandy has provided immense cues that there is immense love between us and she wants to be part of our family. Gobs of issues need to be compromised and resolved. I will offer premarital classes or perform together on line. My life coach has felt strongly that I am ready for a marital relationship.

Many couples do not go through the engagement formality and just enmesh themselves implicitly. On the other extreme is the prince kneeling in front of the princess; and asking the male father for their daughter's hand. I tend to be not that dramatic; but it is respectful to ask the bride's father. Modernly, I would ask both parents for approval. Symbolic aspects such as a ring can occur; but should be by bride and groom agreement. Diamonds are a big deal; and some women may dislike many styles. I am not an expert; though I know Mandy's ring size appears average. I left Janae's ring on her finger signifying our forever union. If I had Janae's ring, I would not utilize it. I decided to finish my golf class followed by picking up kids where the nanny could not help. I will then have our back-up nanny work this evening.

I called Mandy and said I would stop at her house after a required coach's meeting at Highlands Ranch High School. Mandy said great and would have some wine and Hors D'Oeuvres. The symbolic meaning of a marriage proposal would be myself after school at the local jeweler purchasing Colorado's gemstone (mineral beryl in aquamarine). The later engagement diamond cluster we can purchase together. I have positively decided to move forward and ask Mandy's hand in marriage. There is much to do (many steps). I called Mandy's parents and placed them on speaker requesting Mandy's hand in marriage. There was exuberance and crying because they admitted that Mandy wanted this more than anything. We agreed to have a mini-celebration at their house this coming weekend.

My kids were off to school and day care. I picked up the back-up nanny after purchasing the engagement ring with the Colorado Gemstone. It was wrapped beautifully; and the jeweler remarked this was a unique idea. She asked me if I had my speech ready and I said it would be: Mandy, I love you. Will you spend the rest of your life with me? I have got it down. After all the preliminaries and driving to Denver, 2 more coaching opportunities occurred. I kindly said I would contact them over the next couple days. I have not said no to anyone; but will start saying no to many great football jobs regretfully. I appreciate all the great offers. Now is not the time to discuss our 2 QB offensive backfield.
I dressed between formal and informal and knocked on Mandy's door. She said she was still getting ready, but come in. She wanted to know why I was early (sounding suspicious). She came out with a sharp short-sleeve blue summer dress. Again, she asked me why I was an hour early? I stared at her eyes and she sensed a Tsunami was occurring. I placed my arms around her and told her that I loved her forever. I asked her to marry me and spend the rest of her life with myself. She stared at me in happiness, cried, hugged, replied loudly yes, and then asked what was in my hand. She unwrapped the small case with a colorful meaningful bow tie and I placed the Colorado Gem Stone on her finger. Mission accomplished.

Innovations in every sport occur from a fan, coach, or player attempting what has never been athletically accomplished. American sport has witnessed Bill Walsh's West Coast Football Offense, Ben Hogan's successful practical study of the golf swing, NBA's Kiki VanDeWeghe's step back jump shot, the 2002 Miki Ando's (Japan) quadruple jump in women's skating competition, and Hall of Famer Hoyt Wilhelm's standardization of MLB relief pitching. These athletes changed the sport. Prosperous competition at the highest level in your sport requires ingenuity, brilliance, belief, and nearly 24/7 practice. A unique added athletic advantage secures wins. The Colorado Coach's successful development of the 2 QB backfield set has placed America's sport (football) on notice. The Colorado Arsenal offensive attack no longer allows great QB athletes to wear headphones, carry clipboards, and send in play signals from the sidelines. The Colorado Coach has the best team athletes on the field competing rather than "sunning" for years on the bench. The upcoming Colorado Coach Diary II will be a fascinating study of complex practiced innovative football leading to winning gridiron and potential dynasty talk. The upcoming marriage, family life challenges, and robust coaching opportunities are explored in our next diary. Ensure yourself a club seat by following along with the Coloradocoachdiary.com book and podcast and prospective Colorado Coach Diary II.

www.ingramcontent.com/pod-product-compliance
Lightning Source LLC
Chambersburg PA
CBHW072202090426

42740CB00012B/2354